PORTRAIT OF WAGNER

PORTRAIT OF WAGNER

An Illustrated Biography

Hans Mayer

Translated by Robert Nowell

HERDER AND HERDER

1972
HERDER AND HERDER NEW YORK
232 Madison Avenue, New York 10016

Original edition: *Richard Wagner*
in Selbstzeugnissen und Bilddokumenten,
© 1959 by Rowohlt Taschenbuch Verlag GambH, Hamburg

Library of Congress Catalog Card Number: 78–185748
English translation © 1972 by Herder and Herder, Inc.
Manufactured in the United States

CONTENTS

Richard Wagner at Triebschen, 1869.

THE EARLY YEARS

RICHARD WAGNER'S youth and upbringing represented anything but a continuous process of humanistic education. The ninth child of the marriage of Carl Friedrich Wilhelm Wagner, a police official at the Leipzig City Court, he lost his father six months after his birth. Ludwig Geyer, actor, singer, writer, and painter, became Johanna Wagner's second husband. Later Richard Wagner was to describe his stepfather Geyer, as his real "spiritual father." But by the autumn of 1821, when the boy was barely eight and a half years old, Geyer was already dead.

The house where Richard Wagner spent his first years was on the Brühl in Leipzig, very close to the Old Theater. Early in his life the boy came into contact with the theater. He too wanted to become an actor and singer like Geyer; three of his elder sisters had similarly started on a stage career as actresses or singers. After Geyer's death the family moved to Dresden. There, at the Kreuz school, he saw a performance of *Der Freischütz* under Weber's direction which made a great impression on him: he was fascinated by the work itself but also no less by the image of the conductor who stood there and controlled the entire proceedings. Wagner too wanted to be able to stand there some day and hold people in thrall.

He read a great deal, indiscriminately; he listened to a great deal, just as indiscriminately. The thirteen-year-old discovered E. T. A. Hoffmann and Shakespeare for himself, and wrote a schoolboy play called *Leubald* in the style of dramas of chivalry and Shakespeare's tragedies and histories. Thomas Mann has repeatedly pointed out that the characteristics of dilettantism should not go unrecognized in the development of the young Wagner. It is true that Wagner showed no early achievements on a par with the precociousness of Mozart, Mendelssohn, or Schubert. Wagner's early projects in dramatic writing and musical composition were launched on as passionately as they were badly carried out. But all the same they were carried out and brought to a conclusion. Certainly, Wagner's description of the genesis of *Leubald* is reminiscent of schoolboy plays. Nonetheless, Wagner did not merely plan and sketch his play; he completed it. Thanks to his tenacity and frenzy, years of work resulted in a gradual increase in artistic quality, such as at first did not seem possible.

Preoccupation with his school play led to the neglect of his formal studies. Meanwhile the Wagners were living in Leipzig

Wagner's stepfather, Ludwig Heinrich Geyer. Self-portrait.

once again. Richard transferred to the St. Nicholas school, but had to move back a year. This increased his aversion to formal education, while his interest in music grew. He learned the basics of composition, first by teaching himself, then in thorough lessons in musical theory that were broken off too soon.

His chief experience was Beethoven. For him Beethoven's image and music had become an indivisible unity—the artist and his creation: "This image fused in me with that of Shakespeare: in ecstatic dreams I met both of them, saw them and spoke to them; on waking up I was bathed in tears." What is remarkable here is that the experience of literature and the experience of music merge indivisibly into each other. There was no hesitation between literature and another art such as painting or sculpture, as in the case of the young Goethe, Gottfried Keller, or the young Gerhart Hauptmann. Wagner did not waver between two arts: he wanted both at the same time.

The text of *Leubald* was finished, and now the sixteen-year-old schoolboy set his drama to music. At Eastertime 1830 he left school to become a musician, but in the autumn of the same year he had to return to the classroom, where he stayed until February 1831. Then he was released without a diploma, though he obtained permission to be matriculated as a student of music at Leipzig University.

Between his first efforts at drama and music and the end of his formal schooling, a new element entered the scene that was to be decisive for Richard Wagner's intellectual development: politics. In July 1830 the Bourbon regime in Paris was driven out by the people of the French capital in a revolutionary uprising that lasted three days. Even outside France the effects were enormous. There were revolutionary movements in Belgium, Italy, and Spain, and also in many parts of Germany. There were peasant uprisings, occasional mutinies among the troops of small German princedoms, resignations and changes of government at some German courts. In Leipzig there were revolts by the young democrats, particularly the students. Seventeen-year-old Richard Wagner was filled with enthusiasm at the spectacle of revolt and popular resistance to outmoded conditions. But at the same time he was genuinely inspired by the ideas of the movement towards German unity and liberation. Like Heine, Börne, and his contemporary from Hesse, Georg Büchner, he was a supporter of the July revolution. Together with most young and progressive-minded Germans of those days he was an ardent friend of the Polish independence movement. Six years later he was to embody his sharing in the Polish people's struggle in a *Polonia* Overture.

In those years Richard Wagner's reading was almost exclusively determined by the principles of the "Young Germany" movement. In Wilhelm Heinse's novel *Ardinghello* (1785) he discovered an offshoot of the "storm and stress" movement, the prophecy of a principle of life centered on happiness and based on sensual pleasure and this-worldliness. This veneration of sensual pleasure by the Young Germans, the apparent antinomy of "the battle of the sexes," now became for Richard Wagner the basic idea of his first opera to reach the stage, *The Ban on Love,* written in 1835/36. It had been preceded by an opera in the tradition of Weber with the title *The Fairies. The Ban on Love* had one and a half performances in Magdeburg, where Wagner was meanwhile working as conductor: the second night ended— though not for reasons that had anything to do with the opera— with a scandalous fracas among the cast and the abrupt breaking off of the performance. The libretto of *The Ban on Love* had as its source Shakespeare's *Measure for Measure;* but Wagner's text, which otherwise sticks closely to the pattern of the play, differs in one essential point. The character of the Duke disappears—and with him Shakespeare's fundamental problem of justice and the law. Richard Wagner gave the opera the remarkable subtitle

Wagner's mother, Johanne Rosine Wagner, née Pätz. Portrait by Ludwig Heinrich Geyer.

"Grand Comic Opera." For him the center of the stage was held simply by the conflict between uninhibited and inhibited sensuality. In this context the principle of free love is propagated in the ecstatic rejoicing of the finale.

In the following years Richard Wagner continued to be occupied with the synthesis of his fundamental spiritual experiences: his love for Beethoven and Shakespeare, the Young German principle of happiness—and participation in the great movements of liberation of that epoch. In Berlin in 1836 he composed the *Polonia* Overture, a *Britannia* Overture which treated bourgeois England as the then opponent and adversary of the Holy Alliance, and a *Napoleon* Overture. Here too Wagner's close relationship to the political history of his time is unmistakable: it was precisely in those years of 1835 and 1836 that the first new agitation for Bonapartism began in France in opposition to the bourgeois monarchy. And it was at this time that Louis Bonaparte, the later Napoleon III, wrote his *Idées Napoléoniennes.* It is clear that Richard Wagner's creative work was characterized by the taking up and working out of ideas that were then "in the air." In the summer of 1837, when he was working as conductor in Riga—he had married the singer Minna Planer the previous November—he read the English writer Bulwer Lytton's historical novel *Rienzi,* which had been a remarkable success. Between 1837 and 1839 he drew up a libretto on the basis of Lytton's novel and then set it to music on a giant scale. In 1839 he had to flee from his creditors in Riga. Together with his wife and a Newfoundland dog he reached London after an adventurous journey by sailing ship and at the end of August 1839 arrived in France, where he looked up Meyerbeer and then traveled on to Paris. *Rienzi* was completed and Meyerbeer, he hoped, would help him have it performed at the Paris Opera.

From 1839 to 1842 Wagner experienced three years of grim poverty in Paris. He saw bourgeois capitalist society in its developed form: the "poisonous business of money," as Börne had called it, the misery of the ordinary people and the display of affluence of the bankers. He was totally conscious of being the pupil and devotee of classical German art and music, of Goethe and Schiller, Beethoven, and Weber. With this artistic credo he found himself in the middle of an industry that sought to turn all art into merchandise. Here in Paris Richard Wagner collected experiences of the working of society that would influence the whole of his later picture of the world.

In January 1840, through Laube, he became acquainted with Heinrich Heine and took over from him the material for *The Flying Dutchman* and *Tannhäuser.* As a combined acknowledgment of his debt to Beethoven and Goethe he composed his *Faust*

The actress Minna Planer, Wagner's first wife, in stage costume.

Overture, and, when necessity forced him to earn some money by his pen, wrote some short stories on musical subjects after the model of Hoffmann. In these he presented the contrast between genuine art and an environment hostile to art, as in the tales "A Pilgrimage to Beethoven" or "An End in Paris." In Paris he got to know, besides Heine, some of the most important artists of the time; above all it was at this time that he entered upon the acquaintance with Franz Liszt that was to be so significant for his later life.

Meanwhile in Germany, and of course in France too, the philosophy of emancipation had undergone a decisive further development through the work of Ludwig Feuerbach. Feuerbach's *The Nature of Christianity* appeared in 1841 and aroused enthusiasm throughout Europe. This replaced the existing critique of religion by a presentation of the relations between man and religion which sought to reveal all religion as a human and social creation. From now on a new this-worldly religion was to replace "obsolete" Christianity. From now on, too, Richard Wagner was a follower of Feuerbach and an atheist. As late as 1852 he was to write from exile to his friend Uhlig in Dresden: "If you bring me Eduard Devrient's assurance that he is letting God and the immortality of the soul go, then I am prepared to have faith in him. Otherwise all his intellect and will can only aim at preserving God and the soul's survival after death. But what have I got to do with such a person, and what is genuine about him but his cowardice and weakness?" This attitude also provided the seed of the later *Ring of the Nibelung:* the end of the gods and the end of a society based on the domination of gold. Here too Richard Wagner was presenting concrete social experiences.

Early in 1842 he was at last able to return to his native Germany from Paris. *Rienzi* had been accepted for performance in Dresden, and *The Flying Dutchman,* which had meanwhile been completed, was accepted in Berlin. Returning through Thuringia in the spring Richard Wagner caught sight of the Wartburg near Eisenach: Heinrich Heine's theme of Tannhäuser blended with the idea of the song contest on the Wartburg.

Ludwig Feuerbach's substitute religion of human love had been interpreted for himself by Richard Wagner completely in the sense of the Young Hegelians. Wagner's writings on artistic

14

and social reform, especially the pamphlets of 1848, show him, both in their form and their content, as a typical adherent of Stirner's doctrine of "egoism," which despite all apparent contradictions was in its basic ideas identical with Feuerbach's this-worldly ethics. Wagner's rhapsodic essay *The Revolution* of 1849 states: "I want to shatter the power of the overlords, of the law and of property. It is his own will that is man's master, his own pleasure his only law, his own strength his entire property, for it is only the free man that is sacred, and there is nothing higher than he."

While there is immediate documentary evidence for the influences of the Young Germans, and while the effects of Stirner can be shown indirectly, another name must be added to the intellectual experiences of his Paris years. In 1840 Proudhon's book *Qu'est-ce que la propriété?* ("What is Property?") appeared in Paris. As is well known, Proudhon answered the question he had put to himself with the lapidary statement: property is theft. At that time Wagner was living in Paris; he read Proudhon's book and adopted its ideas. While he agreed with Proudhon, his own personal balance sheet was drawn up on the basis of his own experiences and what society in general was going through. In later life he was continually to describe as the two major difficulties in the development of his life the marriage he had entered too young and his lack of inherited wealth. Richard Wagner suffered severely from the fact that it was not possible for him to follow his artistic career "on his own," in economic independence. In Paris Wagner experienced the omnipotence of capital and the epicurean life of financial society, and these impressions too turned him into a disciple of Proudhon. It was here that the basic conception of *The Ring of the Nibelung* was formed, for in quite surprising detail Proudhonism can be traced in Wagner's myth of the changing ownership of the Rhinegold. And the projected drama *Jesus of Nazareth* is unmistakably Proudhonistic. There

Pierre-Joseph Proudhon (1809–1865). Lithograph after a drawing by A. Collette.

we find: "Sins against property arise solely from the law of property." Or again: "Human life is a development in egoism and its renunciation for the sake of the total community." Here Young Hegelian ideas of man's self-alienation are united with Proudhon's ideas whereby this self-alienation is brought about by ownership and property, and finally with Feuerbach's attempt to neutralize this alienation by means of a new ethic of human love.

Here were atheism and utopian ideas of social reform, anti-capitalism and unmistakable characteristics of anarchist individualism. For Wagner did not take over simply Stirner's hostility to law and authority but also the anarchist theses of terrorist "direct action" as a means of fighting the exploiting ruling class. Up to now people have wanted to see merely an accidental acquaintance and meeting in Richard Wagner's and Michail

16

Bakunin's joint involvement in the Dresden uprising of May 1849. Later, especially with regard to Liszt, Richard Wagner was to be at pains to assert his "lack of suspicion" as far as Bakunin's plans were concerned. But at that time the basic ideas of Wagner and Bakunin coincided to a remarkable degree. In Zurich Wagner became a close friend of Georg Herwegh, who was similarly a trusted friend of the Russian anarchist. And it is pure Bakunism when, in a letter to his Dresden friend Uhlig on October 22, 1850, he wrote the following passionate outburst, which Cosima Wagner carefully deleted and the full text of which has only recently become known: "But how will it seem to us when that monstrous city Paris is burned to the ground, when the fire leaps from city to city, when at last in wild enthusiasm they set light to that uncleanable Augean stable to obtain some healthy air? With the fullest presence of mind and without any deceit I assure you that I do not believe any longer in any revolution other than that which starts with the burning of Paris." It should be recalled that this passage was written when Richard Wagner was working on *The Ring of Nibelung*. The burning of Valhalla was therefore in no way understood by Wagner symbolically, but as the experience of direct action aimed at annihilating the corrupt existing society based on egoism and the domination of money.

Richard Wagner's basic political views should in no way be understood as an secondary to his great music dramas. Such a division of the political and the "purely artistic" is explicitly ruled out by the fact that his conscious efforts were above all directed at the unity of artistic form and philosophical content. In actual fact, as far as their intellectual content is concerned, Wagner's great works are closely connected with the development of the Young German, the Young Hegelian, the utopian socialist and anarchist individualist that was Richard Wagner. Besides imaginings of a social or utopian socialist nature, the great music dramas from *Rienzi* to *The Mastersingers* contain at the same time the

17

genuine impulses of a national artist who dreamed of the unification and rise of his fatherland. And beyond this he was able continually to create from the works of the great German writers and composers fresh powers of recovery from his own work.

RIENZI, THE LAST OF THE TRIBUNES

RIENZI was performed at the Dresden Court Opera on October 20, 1842. It started at six in the evening, and the final curtain did not fall until after midnight: already the time scale of the later Wagner operas was being anticipated. Even then it was not the whole of the available score that was performed. It was a tremendous success; on February 1st of the following year Richard Wagner was appointed Royal Saxon conductor with tenure for life. He thus became the successor of Carl Maria von Weber. What he had dreamed of as a boy had come true: he now stood in the same place and before the same orchestra. Minna Wagner's hopes too had at last been fulfilled. From now on she would never tire of urging her husband to write a new *Rienzi* and repeat his success.

But even at the first performance of *Rienzi* Richard Wagner felt profound distaste for his own work. In actual fact it was not until the first performance of *The Mastersingers* on June 21, 1868 in Munich that he was to experience again such a thunderously successful première.

"Grand Tragic Opera in Five Acts" was the subtitle. The librettist-composer knew himself to be under a quite explicit obligation to the spirit of grand opera in the style of Meyerbeer. But grand opera as an art form was inextricably tied up with the financial world of the French bourgeois monarchy, whose aesthetic principles and way of life did not in any way remain restricted to France but were spreading out into Germany. In France grand opera was adapted to the newly arisen wealthy bourgeoisie just as well as two decades later Offenbach's operettas, which tried to offer a combination of enjoyment, social parody and artistic parody, were adapted to the world of the Second Empire. Grand opera represents the invasion of the opera stage by the bourgeois spirit of emulation and the calculating accountants' mentality of the bourgeoisie. It is here that the social basis is found for Wagner's later discussion of this theme of "opera and drama." In grand opera of this type, and so too in *Rienzi,* the court tradition of the eighteenth century opera stage is just as obsolete as the ethical postulates of *Fidelio* or the nationalist coloring of *Der Freischütz.* In each case, the composer's aim was to offer the opera audience something for its money: works of

The first performance of Rienzi at the Royal Court Theater, Dresden, October 20, 1842: the setting of the final scene of Act IV.

inordinate length, continuous opportunities for bravura display, really deep notes for the basses, really high notes for the tenors, really difficult and brilliant coloratura passages for the sopranos. And added to all this were "serious problems" of immediate relevance: Jewish emancipation, religious tolerance, marriage questions.

All this is to be found once again in *Rienzi*. Indeed, in writing the part of Adriano for a contralto, Wagner even goes back to the castrato tradition of the eighteenth century. But this robs the love element of its meaning: the erotic fascination possessed by Mozart's Cherubino is lacking; lacking too is the element of parody linked with the breeches role in *Der Rosenkavalier*. Furthermore, the transvestism in *Figaro* and *Rosenkavalier* is very closely linked with the action, and all this is missing in *Rienzi*. On the purely musical side it must be pointed out in favor of Wagner's decision that he had already written the role of Rienzi for a tenor, so that a second tenor would remain without effect. A contributory element must have been reasons of timbre in duets between Adriano and Irene. All the same it is clear that here we have the librettist and composer giving way before the wishes of the public.

Wagner himself never had any illusions with regard to *Rienzi:* he was aware how superficially he had worked as a composer, despite many brilliant ideas. He was even more strongly aware of the lack of artistic conscientiousness in the putting together of the text. On this point he admits in the introduction to the first volume of his collected writings: "If in the writing of this libretto I had given way only in the slightest degree to the ambition to give myself the airs of a poet, then in keeping with the standard my education had reached, I would probably have been able to appear sufficiently correct, not without some success in diction and verse —something I had already succeeded in doing with the completion of an earlier opera libretto, *The Ban on Love* . . . I find it on the contrary not unenlightening to explore now the reasons that appeared to me when I was writing the text of *Rienzi* to justify such a remarkable neglect of the diction and the verse. These derived from some remarkable observations that I had made at that time on the basis of the operas in our current repertoire. I had discovered that, as long as the subject itself made for effective theater, clumsily and badly translated French and Italian operas made their effect by the sheer poverty of the diction and versification that was presented without any regard for the words and rhymes: whereas the efforts of competent poets to provide the composer with presentable verses and rhymes could never help even the most outstanding, indeed the noblest music to achieve the primary necessity of making its effect as good theater as long as if the piece itself was a failure . . . As I myself was eager for a fortunate success in the theater, I was gripped by complete aversion to the so-called 'fine verses and charming rhymes' that were available to me when I started looking for opera libretti. Instead, I seized each story or novel solely with the intention of carving out of it a sound piece of theater, to be set to a music which in turn would have nothing to do with mere musical rhetorics."

The layout of *Rienzi* follows the conventions of the Meyerbeer tradition. The libretto is simply a mechanical adaptation of Bulwer Lytton's novel, without much regard for artistic or even poetic considerations. But the action and the intellectual content are throughout linked with Wagner's political ideas and with the spirit and atmosphere of the 1830's that were then drawing to a close. The papal notary Cola Rienzi is a man of the people. The Roman nobility is hostile to him. Under the leadership of their tribune the people of Rome—described by Wagner as plebeians—drive the nobles out of the city. Wagner's anti-aristocratic attitude is obvious. Throughout five acts the Colonnas and Orsinis are the embodiment of treachery, bellicosity, assassination. The first art starts straight off with the abduction by lecherous aristocrats of a virgin—Irene, Rienzi's daughter. But the incident with which *Rienzi* begins may not be so strange after all: such an incident was to provide the core of Verdi's *Rigoletto* nine years later. Bourgeois antifeudalism was a familiar attitude to the composers of both *Rienzi* and *Rigoletto*. Another basic element of the literature of bourgeois emancipation also has a role to play: the struggle against ecclesiastical—that is, Catholic —intolerance. Rienzi may succeed in overcoming the Roman nobles, but his fall is brought about by the Pope's hostility and his excommunication, which are represented as the result of a political arrangement between the Emperor and the Pope.

What is however more remarkable is the anticipation of subjects and situations to be found in Wagner's later work. In *Rienzi* the people are shown in a way that is already typical of Wagner. They are the chorus and nothing but the chorus. They either abuse the hero or acclaim him impartially. The way in which the people either support or betray Rienzi throughout the five acts points forward to the knights who are to appear later in *Lohengrin,* where their choral and musical role is of great importance but where their contribution to the action remains restricted to the acclamation of a sometimes fairly rapid change of dukes: Telramund, Lohengrin, Gottfried of Brabant. This has nothing to do simply with musical or dramaturgical considerations but is essentially concerned with political matters. *Rienzi* hovers curiously between rebellion and obstinate conservatism: revolution—but only when demanded from above; The fight for freedom—"but dignified, without frenzy."

Musically this grand opera is throughout in the tradition of the species: arias, ensembles, effective choruses and marches, the best known being the song of the messengers of peace, a battle hymn after the model of Meyerbeer's *Les Huguenots,* a grand ballet-pantomime in the usual place in the second act. Scenically, too, a great deal is offered: abduction, corpses, attempts at murder, Rienzi on horseback, the Lateran and the Capitol, finally the burning and collapse of the Capitol. Certainly more than a scenic effect was envisaged when the end of this opera anticipates the end of the greatest of the later music dramas, the *Ring* cycle. The burning of the Capitol and Rienzi's downfall—the burning of Valhalla and the downfall of Wotan and his gods.

Certainly it is not unreasonable to point to such examples of continuity, for later the composer of *Rienzi* was only too concerned to differentiate this grand tragic opera from his later work. In the introduction to his collected writings he wrote: "As far as my knowledge goes, I am not capable of discovering in the life of any artist such a striking transformation accomplished in so short a time as that which is here shown in the case of the composer of those two operas, of which the first had hardly been completed before the second was almost ready. But the cognate characteristics of both works should without a doubt not escape anyone who examines them carefully. The need for effective theater certainly underlies *The Flying Dutchman* no less than *The Last of the Tribunes*. It is only that everyone will surely feel that something significant had happened to the man who wrote them: perhaps a profound shock, in any case a violent change, to which longing and loathing contributed equally. I would like to hope that *The German Musician in Paris* will provide sufficient elucidation of this point."

Between *Rienzi* and the *Dutchman* lay the years of poverty in Paris, the experience of the world of the bourgeois monarchy.

THE FLYING DUTCHMAN

HEINRICH HEINE's fragment "From the Memoirs of Herr von Schnabelewobski" was written in 1831 and published three years later in the first volume of his *Salon*. In it Heine told the story

23

Heinrich Heine.

of the flying Dutchman. It was not his own invention, he said: his aim was merely to recount a play seen in Holland. This may have been true; the material of the story was at that time quite generally known in European literature and was a favorite theme. Nevertheless it is obvious that Richard Wagner took the entire plot from Heine or from Heine's model.

As a conductor in Riga Wagner had read Heine's story—shortly before he and Minna had to flee from their creditors there. With the help of smugglers they reached Pillau; from there an old sailing ship, the *Thetis,* was to take the two fugitives and their enormous dog, together with the crew of seven, to London. In the Skagerrak a terrible storm overtook them and drove them towards Norway, where they found shelter in a bay. The sailors, rejoicing over their deliverance, sang a sea shanty. What he had seen and heard mingled in Wagner's vision with his memories of what he had read: the sounds of the sailors' song, the terrifying sight of the raging sea, the memory of Heine's tale of the ghost ship and the flying Dutchman. Wagner stopped in London to hand Lord Bulwer Lytton a copy of the libretto he had written on the basis of his novel *Rienzi,* but the novelist-statesman was not available. Then in the years of poverty in Paris, between requests for financial aid and visits to people connected with the opera and influential patrons, the text was written for a romantic opera on the subject of the Dutchman.

For Wagner the cruelest irony of life at that time in the Paris of the bourgeois monarchy lay undoubtedly in the fact that, while the director of the opera, Léon Pillet, was ready to accept the interesting idea of an opera on the ghost ship, even though in France this was no longer quite a novelty, he merely shrugged his shoulders at the proposal that the librettist Wagner be entrusted with setting the text to music. Wagner finally sold his rights in the libretto for five hundred francs—with the internal reservation that he would set the work in its German verse form for the German stage in a way that would correspond to the vision he had seen and heard of the sea and the Norwegian fjord.

It was thus that the music of the *Dutchman* was written in Paris, in seven weeks. With the five hundred francs Wagner was able to buy a piano. First to occur to him was the idea of the helmsman's song, which began unaccompanied in a naïve and wholly unoperatic manner to rise up and then die away in natural rustlings with emphasis on the octave, with support by the tremolo typical of the orchestration of the *Dutchman.* Then the spinning song was composed. By the time Wagner received the news that *Rienzi* had been accepted by Dresden, he was ready to take the score of the *Dutchman* with him on the journey.

The first performance of *The Flying Dutchman,* "A Romantic Opera in Three Acts," took place at the Royal Saxon Court Theater, Dresden, on Monday, January 2, 1843, less than three months after the first performance of *Rienzi.* It was a *succès*

Playbill for the first performance of *The Flying Dutchman*.

d'estime, hardly anything more. The public had naturally expected a counterpart to *Rienzi* and so were disillusioned. Nevertheless the fact that the première of the *Dutchman* was only half a success was no longer an absolutely vital matter for Wagner: his appointment as first conductor at the Royal Opera could serve as compensation.

Both of Wagner's statements about the *Dutchman* are correct. He could declare both that it was intended as a piece of effective theater just as *Rienzi* was, and that nevertheless he had created a work of "violent change" in his romantic opera, which no longer bore the subtitle "grand opera." The *Dutchman* is first of all in the German romantic operatic tradition—in its contrasts of material and spirit as well as in the musical means applied. As was almost always the case with the plots of German romantic operas, the conflict between the world of mankind and the world of spirits provides the intellectual core of the work. E. T. A. Hoffman's opera *Undine,* after the short story by Baron de la Motte Fouqué, was intended to follow this basic principle; *Der Freischütz* and *Oberon* had dealt with this conflict no less than the operas of Heinrich Marschner. Part of this tradition was that man's encounter with the spirit world, entered on in a spirit of friendship and confidence, had to end tragically. Long before Wagner the mingling of the two spheres occurred as the meeting of love and death.

The conflict of the human with the spirit world in the context of the love-death theme thus provided one element from tradition. A second was to be found in the concept of *Weltschmerz.* The character of the Dutchman as drawn by Richard Wagner is not simply an embodiment of the spirit world. He is rather an extension into the spirit world of the outsider burdened by *weltschmerz.* The sceptical and anti-social character of the rebel reduced to resignation was continually evoked by the boldest and most genuinely rebellious artists of European romanticism, which in both its political aims and its artistic forms of expression is essentially distinct from the German romantic school. People have often talked of "Byronism," since Byron's *Cain* or *Manfred* could serve as models for this literature.

The Dutchman in Richard Wagner's characterization is not simply the incarnation of someone accursed: he means far more than what Heine had seen in the "wandering Jew of the ocean." Wagner's Dutchman is accursed, but above all he is sick and weary of mankind and human society. Among other things he is

27

also a misanthrope in the classical dramatic tradition which was already beginning to affect literature again from 1830 onwards.

The linking of the two motives—the contrast between the world of men and the world of spirits and the theme of *Weltschmerz*—gives rise to a conflict which Wagner had not yet plumbed to the depths. The oath of everlasting loyalty given by Senta can only refer to the faithfulness of married love, to an earthly life shared faithfully with her beloved. But the Dutchman has to understand this oath in quite a different way. He needs Senta's everlasting loyalty in order to be able to die. The conflict is insoluble. At this point the *Dutchman* extends beyond all its literary and operatic models: for the first time a typical Wagnerian problem appears on the opera stage.

The *Dutchman, Tannhäuser* and *Lohengrin* have as much to differentiate them from each other as they have in common. But they are all dramas about artists involving almost the same situation. What is involved is always a conflict between the genius and the customary concepts of life, art and morals to be found in the world he lives in. Tannhäuser's artistic leanings come into conflict with traditional ideas about art and the way it should be practised. But the artists characterized in the Dutchman and Lohengrin are figures of geniuses who without demonstration or investigation come forward with absolute and unconditional claims. The artist, the genius, demand loyalty without question or proof, simply because of their life as genius, as intellect. The Dutchman, Tannhäuser, and Lohengrin contain autobiographical elements just as much as do Wagner's later characters of Stolzing and Sachs, Tristan, Wotan, and Amfortas.

The music of the *Dutchman* also marks a transition between the traditional and what is completely new. The score is laid out according to the traditional operatic numbers: overture, then the first act with an introduction, the helmsman's song, recitative and aria, scene and duet, final chorus. In the other two acts we also encounter the customary forms of romantic opera, the ballade,

Part of the stage setting for the third act of *The Flying Dutchman* at the 1956 Bayreuth Festival.

aria, cavatina, duets and trios, finales with the chorus that follow all the rules. The harmonic language of romanticism is extensively adopted and retained: the diminished sevenths of Weber, Mendelssohn, or Marschner appear useful even to the composer of the *Dutchman*. At the same time there appears a chromaticism of a boldness that goes far beyond all available models.

The further development of the Weber song and choral number is extraordinary. The spinning song and the sailors' chorus are top melodic ideas in the folk song style: they have made an essential contribution to the opera's undiminished popularity. But juxtaposed with these numbers in the style of folksong, and not always organically connected with them, are melodic developments that evoke an affinity with Meyerbeer and with the young Verdi. An example is the D major aria of Daland in the second act.

The overture remains almost unparalleled. It is a symphonic poem, but unlike Beethoven or Weber, it does not simply take the major themes and the musical and intellectual contrasts of the opera and link them into a self-enclosed orchestral piece. The overture to the *Dutchman* is in fact an anticipation of the entire plot. In this way it marks itself off from the overture to *Tannhäuser* and from the preludes to *Lohengrin, Tristan,* or *Parsifal.* It was only in the prelude to the *Mastersingers* that Wagner again provided a complete musical presentation of the plot of the opera.

TANNHÄUSER

TANNHÄUSER too arose from a combination of visual impressions and literary reminiscences. Wagner's early reading included *The Serapion Brothers* by Hoffmann, and through this he came to know the story of the singers' contest that opens the third section of this work. Inspired by Hoffmann, who had drawn his knowledge of the epic song contest from the chronicle by Johann Christian Wagenseil but who did not know the Middle High German poem on the Wartburg contest, Richard Wagner turned to the documents of German medieval poetry and folk song. This too arose from the protest of the German musician in Paris against the way in which the world of the bourgeois monarchy treated art as a business and turned it into merchandise. The literary creations of the German nineteenth century had aroused in Wagner the curiosity to go back to the original medieval sources of this later literature. So the road from Hoffmann led back to the Middle High German poem on the Wartburg contest.

But the text of this poem knew hardly anything of Tannhäuser or the Venusberg. Even in Hoffmann's tale Heinrich von Ofterdingen stood in the place which later Wagner was to yield to the character of Tannhäuser in his romantic opera. The Tannhäuser-Venus theme had its own particular genesis and tradition. There was only a mild hint in the medieval folksong of Tannhäuser to point the way to the cycle of sagas about the Wartburg and the singers' contest.

The Tannhäuser theme was then also offered to Wagner by Heinrich Heine. *Tannhäuser: A Legend* was written by Heine in 1836 and later included in the collection of his *New Poems.* Heine wrote as if he possessed a more recent reworking of the Tannhäuserlied. At that time, in the first decades of the nineteenth century, there were many opportunities for a German to become acquainted with the Tannhäuser saga: through Arnim, Brentano, and *The Youth's Magic Horn,* through the *German Legends* of the Grimm brothers, and through an older version of the saga of the Venusberg that Ludwig Bechstein had published in 1835 in his *Treasury of Thuringian Legends.*

Heine took over the theme of Tannhäuser's separation from the Lady Venus and then depicted the pilgrimage to Rome under-

31

The harmony was complete. The Thuringian landscape in spring, the Tannhäuser theme and the recollection of the Hoffmann tale of the singers' contest were fused into one another.

From the start the Tannhäuser theme predominated. *The Venusberg* was the original title of the new libretto. The reason why Wagner chose a different title—*Tannhäuser and the Song Contest on the Wartburg*—three years later, when he was sending the vocal score off to be printed, is similarly recounted in his autobiography. C. F. Meser of Dresden, who was publishing the work at Wagner's expense, had taken offense at the title *The Venusberg* ("Mount of Venus"): "He asserted I did not mix with the public and did not hear how people were making the most revolting jokes about this title, jokes which in his view must originate from the staff and students of the medical clinic in Dresden, since they related to a type of obscenity current only in these circles. It was enough to have pointed out to me how great an obstacle this trivial matter provided to persuade me to make the alteration he wished; I used the name of my hero Tannhäuser to provide a title for that saga material that I had linked up with the Tannhäuser myth to which I had originally been a stranger, a combination which later was to annoy the scholar and recounter of sagas, Simrock, whom I valued so very highly."

The genesis of Tannhäuser thus falls within the early Dresden period. The scenario itself was written down in the early summer of 1842, at Teplitz. Then Wagner had to interrupt work on the opera, since the autumn was to be occupied with the first performances of *Rienzi* and the *Dutchman* at Dresden. Roughly a year after that springtime vision in Thuringia, in April 1843, the text was ready. Wagner had already made some first musical sketches in Teplitz. It is interesting that in this case once again it should be the element of folk song that occurred as the first musical idea. The composition of *The Flying Dutchman* had

34

begun with the helmsman's song and the spinning song. This time the first idea was the shepherd's spring song. It was the Venusberg music which, on his own admission, gave the composer the greatest difficulties. All Wagner's later revisions of the *Tannhäuser* score were extensively devoted to this bacchanal music and to the structural relationship between the overture and the Venusberg music.

The actual work of composition was completed in Dresden before the end of 1844, and the full score was written out in the first months of 1845. And for this work too the first performance ensued in Dresden. Three years after the première of *Rienzi* in the same theater the première of *Tannhäuser* took place on October 19, 1845 at the Saxon Court Opera. Once again Richard Wagner conducted from the podium where Carl Maria von Weber had stood. Wilhelmine Schröder–Devrient, who was a firm believer in Wagner's genius, had taken on the highly dramatic but thankless role of Venus. Elisabeth was sung by Johanna Wagner, niece of the librettist, composer and conductor. The difficult role of Tannhäuser, which arouses alarm in singers to this day, was sung by the tenor Tichatschek. It was above all to his failure that Wagner ascribed the fact that this première at Dresden provided again"no more than a *succès d'estime.*" Moreover the actual conclusion of the opera was still remarkably rudimentary in this first Dresden version: Venus did not reappear, Elisabeth's corpse was not brought on stage, the young pilgrims did not arrive with the staff that was putting forth green leaves. The final scene obviously relied very heavily on an audience that was capable of understanding mere hints. Wagner was therefore right to develop further his original version and give the opera the conclusion we know today.

There were difficulties too in training the singers of the time in the entirely new ways of acting and singing that *Tannhäuser* now rather peremptorily demanded of them. How difficult this was

35

can be grasped if one reads the comprehensive essay Wagner wrote in exile in Zurich: "On the Performance of *Tannhäuser: A Communication to the Conductors and Performers of This Opera.*" Wagner must have acquired the most bitter experiences to have been forced to make the following declaration: "It is blatantly obvious that in this way gifted dramatic compositions must be irredeemably distorted beyond recognition. But it is equally clear that even the most superficial modern Italian operas would gain enormously in performance if that cohesion—which exists even in these operas, although only in the most grotesque outlines—came into play. I must however state that a dramatic composition like my *Tannhäuser,* whose only chance of making its effect lies purely in that cohesion between the dramatic action and the music, will at once be destroyed if the behavior I have complained of on the part of conductor and director is applied. I therefore request conductors who are led by inclination or duty to perform my work, first of all to read the score in no other way than with the most careful regard for the words of the libretto and finally for the numerous detailed directions with regard to the action on the stage."

The plot of *Tannhäuser* and all the chief characters were already to be found in prototype in the medieval sources and in the modern writers such as Hoffman and Heine who had stimulated Wagner's interest in the subject. Nevertheless something completely new arose from the fusion of the two sources and themes, not simply in the writing of the music but also in the ideas that form the drama's intellectual content and in the characters themselves. The medieval idea of the singers' contest had as its aim the glorification of the prince. This aspect of the traditional models had its aftereffects even in Hoffmann's tale, though with some decisive changes. In his version, the outsider Heinrich von Ofterdingen was as a "burgher of Eisenach" contrasted with the five other singers, "all of knightly rank." Admittedly, too, in Hoff-

Richard Wagner, Paris, 1842. Drawing by E. B. Kietz.

mann's story the double aspect of heavenly and earthly love plays a part, for the sorcerer Nasias sings a "song of the beautiful Helen and the boundless joys of the Venusberg," against which Wolfram had set the "heavenly bliss of the pure love of the devout minstrel." All the same this was not quite the main point as far as Hoffmann was concerned. In his singers' contest the antithesis rested on the conflict between a poetry based on natural

37

perception and experience and an artificial, learned poetic craft. Hoffmann, too, did not work out his characters as representatives of ideas with very much logical consistency.

Wagner on the other hand makes an explicit contrast between the two forms of sensual and spiritual, lower and higher love. Since he fused the Wartburg theme with the Tannhäuser theme, he had to give the Lady Venus an ideal counterpart. In this way the work focused on the contrast between the pagan goddess and the Christian saint. This corresponded to the medieval view of things, of course, but also belonged very explicitly to ideas inherited from the Young Germany movement. Venus and Elisabeth represented the pagan and the Christian world, but in the view of the Young German writers there was also embodied in this the classical conflict between delight in the senses and peace of mind, between pagan sensuality and Christian asceticism. The conflict, which was closely connected with the emancipation of the bourgeoisie from Lutheran moral theology, was understood by Heinrich Heine as the opposition between the Hellenic world that delighted in sensuality and the ascetic Nazarene. Heine's views were also known to Wagner. But he did not understand the saintly element in Elisabeth in a genuinely Christian manner: the character represented pure asceticism, the denial of the senses. This once again was connected with E. T. A. Hoffmann, whose tales and stories had denied any sensual fulfillment to the artist in love.

The writer of *Tannhäuser* was later to remark that his drama was really to be understood as what we would now call an "abreaction." Wagner, himself sexually unfulfilled, became enraptured with the lofty and sublimated images of the Venusberg. Only he made Tannhäuser both become guilty and feel his guilt. Here too the tragic dénouement was given a note of inexorability.

The Young German literary credo had already been met by

the fact that Tannhäuser hovered between love in its lower and higher forms, between paganism and Christianity, and was convinced by this conflict. But Wagner understood the conflict in a different and more individual manner. The fundamental problem of the work is indicated in a very detailed and important letter to Liszt which was written in Zurich on May 29, 1852, and which contains precise detailed instructions for a performance of *Tannhäuser:* "To begin with, everything is grouped around Elisabeth, the mediator: *she* has taken the center of the stage and everyone is content merely to listen to her or to repeat what she has been saying. Then Tannhäuser, who is becoming aware of the outrageous crime he has committed, falls into the most terrible contrition; and—when he again finds words with which to express himself, words which are first still denied to him, since he lies as if unconscious on the ground—*he* suddenly becomes the single most important character, and everything now is grouped around him as it was formerly around Elisabeth. Everything that is superfluous now withdraws into the background, everything to a certain extent hinges on him as he sings:

> To lead the sinner to salvation
> God's messenger came near to me,
> but with wicked intentions
> I raised my impious gaze to her.
> You high above this earth
> who sent me the angel of my salvation,
> have mercy on me who, plunged in sin,
> failed to recognize the mediator of grace.

In this stanza and this aria is to be found the whole meaning of Tannhäuser's catastrophe: indeed, the whole essence of Tannhäuser, everything that for me makes him such an impressive and moving figure, is expressed here alone. All his suffering, his painful pilgrimage, everything flows from the meaning of this stanza: without this being understood as it must be understood at this point, and precisely at this point, Tannhäuser as a whole remains inexplicable, a capricious, hesitant—pitiable figure."

What Wagner perceived as Tannhäuser's guilt suddenly becomes clear. The basis of his tragedy is not that he stayed in the Venusberg. But to project sensual desires onto Elisabeth, to fail to recognize "the mediator of grace" and strive to possess her: this is the basis of Tannhäuser's inexpiable guilt.

Thus in this romantic opera there is a remarkable adoption of the classical theme and conflict. A further fundamental aspect similarly often goes unrecognized even though Richard Wagner explicitly indicated it. When he sent the completed score of *Tannhäuser* to Karl Gaillard in Berlin, he wrote in the accompanying letter, dated June 5, 1845: "I am sending you herewith my Tannhäuser, the very image and embodiment of him; a German from head to toe; accept him in friendship as a present. May he be capable of winning me the hearts of my German fellow countrymen to a greater extent! This work must be good, otherwise I can never do anything that is any good. In writing it I was under a genuine spell; whenever I was dealing with my material I trembled in glowing warmth; when it came to the long interruptions that divided me from my work I was always with one breath re-immersed in the peculiar atmosphere that enraptured me when the idea first came into my head."

The language he uses is a little astonishing. In what way is the minstrel Tannhäuser "a German from head to toe"? One would much sooner claim this description for Wolfram and Tannhäuser's other opponents in the contest on the Wartburg whom Wolfram undertakes to praise.

Nevertheless Wagner emphasizes precisely the German side of Tannhäuser's nature. Here too there is a fusion of social experience with highly personal problems. Tannhäuser's hesitation between Venus and Elisabeth is, as has been indicated, connected with the personal inner life of Richard Wagner as a man and as

40

an artist. But from another point of view Tannhäuser does not simply represent the character of an artist but the character of an artist with autobiographical touches drawing on the experience of the artist Richard Wagner. The German side of the natures of both Tannhäuser and Richard Wagner is particularly noticeable at the renunciation of Venus and the world of the Venusberg. The profound effect achieved on the stage every time the world of Venus becomes paler and more insubstantial and the Thuringian spring landscape emerges does not depend simply on the theatrical effect of the change of decor but on the change from one mental world to another.

Wagner was right to demand—in a letter to Liszt (January 1852)—that Tannhäuser was to sing all three stanzas of his song in the Venusberg: "Otherwise the correct crescendo of felling—in its effect on Venus—will be completely lost." The first stanza of Tannhäuser's song begs for release from a pleasure that has become cloying. The second stanza contains a more powerful argument: longing for the German landscape. Suddenly Tannhäuser has taken on the form of the German musician in Paris, Richard Wagner. The Venusberg and the pattern of life in Paris, the German landscape and the longing for Germany: these now coincide, and it is in this way that Tannhäuser, and not Wolfram, is primevally German.

Even the attraction of the grotto of love can no longer hold Tannhäuser captive: the third stanza of his song makes use of the heroic key of E flat major known from Beethoven. Tannhäuser appears in a new guise, with new aspects of the national feelings of German artists:

> But I must go from here to the world of earth:
> with you I can only become a slave.
> It is freedom I want,
> freedom I thirst for,
> and I will endure battle and conflict

41

Tannhäuser returns to the Venusberg. Drawing by Aubrey Beardsley.

> even if it means death and destruction.
> So from your realm I must flee—
> Queen, goddess, let me go.

The composer insisted that the true conflict in *Tannhäuser* be made clear scenically towards the end of the second act, and demanded that the crescendo of feeling in Tannhäuser's song be grasped.

Moreover, as far as the music is concerned a characteristic expression is found for the German side of Tannhäuser's nature. It can be demonstrated that Richard Wagner was accustomed to expressing the markedly German sections of his works by means of music of a march character. This was something that began long before *The Mastersingers*. If one looks at the rhythm of Tannhäuser's song one cannot mistake the character of hymnlike march music. It cannot of course be denied that similar passages in the score—including these stanzas of Tannhäuser's song—are at the same time very close to the *bel canto* style of grand opera and especially too of Italian opera. The great D major cantilena for baritone, which is begun by Wolfram when he meets Tannhäuser again and which is then broadened into a sextet by the four other minstrels joining in as well as the Landgrave, is an example of an outstanding melodic idea; but it remains quite unmistakably embedded in the tradition of the French and Italian opera stage.

Nevertheless the German and non-German spiritual worlds, only externally embodied in Venus and Elisabeth, are expressed in music of the most extreme contrast. This is precisely where the originality lies in the score of *Tannhäuser*. Here too there is a remarkable ambivalence in the musical approach, and one that is characteristic of Wagner. In the libretto the French and pagan world of the Venusberg is to be overcome by the German landscape, by the ideal of German art, by purity and holiness. But the musical expression of this Germanness, of German courtly love and the knightly tradition, is abundantly conservative, not to say routine. The pilgrims' chorus and the type of songs Wolfram sings possess a fatal similarity to the minor German composers of men's part-songs who were the successors of romanticism in music.

In contrast, Wagner provided the world of Venus with music of the utmost originality which, in its rhythmic complexity, imaginative harmony, and novelty of orchestration, marks a step beyond anything that had been created by him before. The stiff and stolid rhythms of the pilgrims' chorus or the customary German romantic cantilena are broken and everything seems to glide; the unequivocal character of the underlying tonality seems to have been blotted out, and what was dark tremolo in the orchestra of the *Dutchman* has changed into a fluttering tremolo of the strings; figurations flare up like bursts of flame. The unequivocal eroticism of the rhythmic movement is already supported by chromatically rising sextolets in the celli in the Venusberg section of the overture; a bar starts with a *forte* only to drop back at once into *piano*. But when—once again in the overture—this unequivocal music of debauchery then changes over to Tannhäuser's song to Venus, this may mean a powerful increase in intensity from the musical point of view, but at the same time it marks a transition from the writing, intangible sound world of the Lady Venus to the German march style of the song of praise by Tannhäuser, the German musician in Paris.

Was Wagner aware that the musical contrast between Wolfram and Tannhäuser was taken as an antithesis between the music of the romantic epigoni and the new music of Wagner

Caricature by Gill in *Eclipse*.

himself? There is much in favor of this view. The uneasiness aroused in Mendelssohn and Robert Schumann by the score of *Tannhäuser* was not unjustified: they must have felt themselves attacked personally.

With the appearance of *Tannhäuser* and its slowly but steadily increasing popularity arose the conflict between Wagnerians and anti-Wagnerians. Ten years after the first performance the opera had already been staged in most German opera houses: it had been played in Riga, too, where Wagner had once had to suffer as a conductor and dodge his creditors; *Tannhäuser* was performed in Prague, in Antwerp, in Strasbourg. The fronts of supporters and embittered opponents began to form. The writer-composer had now become so well known that he could offer a rewarding subject for parodists. Johann Nestroy had not been able to avoid appropriating Hebbel's *Judith. Tannhäuser,* and later *Lohengrin,* also struck him as offering an abundant opportunity for parody.

The growing success of *Tannhäuser* also marks the opening of an almost inexhaustible chapter on "Richard Wagner in Caricature." Prominent first were the Berlin press and periodicals, since it was only in 1856 that it was possible to put *Tannhäuser* on at the Prussian Court Opera in Berlin. On that occasion *Kladderadatsch* published a whole page of caricatures which still were directed almost more against the "Abbé" Franz Liszt than against Wagner and were aiming at the charge of religious "proselytization." But despite its narrow-minded petty bourgeois outlook *Kladderadatsch* did not misunderstand the real intellectual and artistic standpoints. It also outguessed Nietzsche, since it was *Tannhäuser* and not first *Parsifal* that inaugurated the "Wagner Case."

LOHENGRIN

WITH the appearance of *Lohengrin* the argument between Wagnerians and anti-Wagnerians grew more intense. Today *Lohengrin* is perhaps the work of Wagner that arouses the strongest differences of opinion. The impetus of the *Dutchman* has prevailed, *The Mastersingers* and *Tristan* have similarly retired from the fray, while *Parsifal* was conceived as an exception to the Wagnerian *œuvre* and has remained an exception on the opera stage to this day. Complete performances of the *Ring,* too, are relatively rare; following a general law of musical success, this cycle falls into popular and less sought-after sections, one could almost say into pleasant and unpleasant parts: to the first category belong the first act of *The Valkyrie,* the ride of the Valkyries, the forging song and the forest murmurs, while in the second, to the sorrow of what Bernard Shaw termed the "perfect Wagnerite," belongs the entire mythology of the *Ring.* And the popular arias, choruses, and orchestral excerpts of *Tannhäuser* are in the old operatic tradition.

These too are to be found in *Lohengrin,* perhaps to a much greater extent than in its predecessor. Nevertheless any discussion of *Lohengrin* is always liable to turn easily into an argument between supporters and opponents. Faced with *Tristan* and even with the *Ring,* it is possible to distinguish purely musical enjoyment from unease over the work's psychology, implied philosophy and mythology. But with *Lohengrin* enjoyment of the music increases the total effect of unease—as if this enchanting music shared in the responsibility.

There is no need to recall the recent past of Germany or the juxtaposition of *Lohengrin* and Hitler's Third Reich for *Lohengrin* to bring to light questionable elements in Wagner's art. Rapture and hatred crowd in close on one another to an extent that is rare elsewhere with regard to works of art, even those by Richard Wagner. The effect of *Lohengrin* on the Bavarian Crown Prince Ludwig, who already at the age of twelve had devoured Wagner's essay *The Work of Art of the Future* and who heard the opera when he was barely sixteen, was magical: he listened to the opera in tears and fell completely under its spell. The miracle of *Lohengrin* was to repeat itself in Wagner's life. The opera provided the basis for a strange relationship, that productive yet portentous friendship based ultimately on misunderstanding, between the prematurely aged composer and the boyish king who was not really musical.

A straight line leads from *Tannhäuser* to *Lohengrin:* they are very close both in the period of their conception and in the mental climate they inhabit. The basic idea of *Lohengrin* was worked out in July 1845, at the same time that the idea of *The Mastersingers* first began to take shape. *Lohengrin* carries on where *Tannhäuser* left off, while Lohengrin and Stolzing are both legitimate relations of the minstrel Tannhäuser. Wagner's theme of the artist and the historical significance of the Wagnerian artist had remained too wrapped up in the mists of legend in *Tannhäuser.* It seemed necessary to continue the conflict in a region of history that was geographically and historically more credible. Wagnerian and anti-Wagnerian art, Tannhäuser and Wolfram, would no longer be relegated to the legendary Middle Ages but would be related to the authentic and historical Germany of sixteenth-century Nuremberg. And besides the historical aspect of the sixteenth century the political aspect of the nineteenth century in Germany and in particular the year 1845 is seen in the first draft of the scenario for *The Mastersingers* which

47

Wagner wrote at Marienbad on July 16, 1845. He had already worked out the two concluding lines:

> Even if the holy Roman empire should vanish,
> we shall still have our holy German art.

But side by side with the first draft for *The Mastersingers* were historical and political sections of Lohengrin such as:

Place hosts ready for battle on the land that bears the German name, then no one will again abuse the German realm.

Or:

> Great king, allow me to prophesy:
> a great victory is granted to you who are pure.
> Even in the most distant days to come,
> the eastern hordes will never invade Germany victoriously.

But once again it will not do to interpret such statements simply in the light of our own experience. First of all they must be understood within the context of the time when they were written. And here again the connection with *The Mastersingers* is seen—as is the connection with *Tannhäuser*. *Tannhäuser* was a matter of German legend and medieval poetry. The legendary character and the historical vagueness of the romantic view of the Middle Ages were retained by Richard Wagner. But in his case the landscape was more tangible. Lohengrin too, who like the Dutchman and Tannhäuser or even Stolzing is an artist, and is in addition an ideal, remains a legendary figure. Wagner had found him in Wolfram von Eschenbach, who had described the knight of the swan, Parzival's son, as Loherangrin. The poem of the minstrels' contest similarly indicates connections with the Lohengrin theme. At the end of the thirteenth century a separate Lohengrin epic was written in Bavaria. This set the tale in the

Ludwig II as King Lohengrin. Caricature from *Der Floh*.

time of King Henry I of Saxony and the war against Hungary
and the Saracens. At Marienbad Wagner read the Lohengrin epic
in Joseph von Görres's edition with its ample introduction. Here
everything was at hand: German legend but much more closely
connected with German history than in the case of Tannhäuser;
German history with the possibility of contemporary political
relevance; and in addition the possibility of finding a fresh form
for the artist theme. The libretto and music of *Lohengrin* were
written in the three years that led up to the revolution of 1848.
The score was completed at the end of March that year, one
month after the outbreak of the French February revolution,

49

two weeks after the March outbreaks in Berlin and Vienna and after the outbreak of the revolution in Saxony.

Lohengrin is once again Tannhäuser, once again the artist, once again Richard Wagner. He is the miracle, the genius, who appears in the midst of everyday life. The genius figures of the German "Storm and Stress" movement were independent and self-sufficient: as artists their genius covered the fields both of action and of rebellion. The romantics had replaced the artist as genius by the artist as miracle, with a religious aura surrounding him. Here Wagner did not follow them. Romanticism may be an extensive requirement in *Lohengrin,* but it is not the essence. *Tristan* is much more romantic than *Lohengrin.* The miracle of the Grail and of Lohengrin as a character has been secularized, though not yet understood in a Christian sense. The composer of *Lohengrin* interpreted the Grail quite differently from the later composer of *Parsifal.* In his *Communication to my Friends* Wagner let no doubt remain on this score: "Nor is *Lohengrin* in any way a work that has grown out of the Christian view of things, but is one that has its roots deep in human history: it is a common but fundamental error of our superficial way of looking at things when we take the specifically Christian view as somehow providing the original creative force. None of the most characteristic and most moving Christian myths originally belong specifically to the Christian spirit as we usually understand it: all of them had been passed down to it from the purely human view of things that preceded it and were merely worked over according to its individual peculiarities."

Wagner cannot use an authentically medieval Lohengrin, since it is the problems not of the Christian artist but simply of the artist that create Lohengrin's tragic isolation. He is the miraculous in a world which (in the form of Elsa) may long for the miraculous but is also concerned to force it into the sphere of everyday life and even thus to strip it of what is miraculous about it. As in *The Flying Dutchman,* as in the German romantic tradition, there is once again a link between the world of men and the world of spirits, but this link must end tragically. The marriage of Lohengrin and Elsa is just as much doomed to failure as is the betrothal of Senta to the Ahasuerus of the oceans. To this is added Tannhäuser's protest against the commonplace nature of the surrounding world and the way it turns art into a business. The artist Tannhäuser longs for joys and griefs other than those desired by Wolfram and Walther—so he enters the Venusberg to reach a new artistic world. Lohengrin *is* this new artist, this Wagner or Wagnerian. The glory surrounding the knighthood of the Grail offers merely the external form to be taken by the symbol of the artist, but it is not this symbol itself. Lohengrin represents the artistic world that is based on what is exceptional, that will not let itself be forced back into the commonplaces of everyday life. This situation is ingeniously expressed by Lohengrin's forbidding Elsa to question him. Genius demands unquestioning loyalty, profoundest trust, all the prerogatives of the extraordinary. Everyday life demands to know names and categories, wants the miraculous fitted into the customary. This conflict had already shattered E. T. A. Hoffmann's artist characters. Lohengrin on the other hand cannot simultaneously fill the roles of knight of the Grail, husband and duke. The Grail is utopia, which cannot be reduced to everyday life. Hence Lohengrin's conflict must necessarily end tragically. And this is all the more so since Wagner was basically inclined to regard the surrounding world and everyday life as what is unnatural but to see the miracle of the artist as a higher kind of naturalness.

Wagner as librettist provided two foundations for the special tragedy of Lohengrin and Elsa that arises and must arise from this conflict. In the first place it springs from Elsa's guilt: she had tried to force the miraculous into sensual existence. In his *Communication to my Friends* Wagner describes the reasons for the impossibility of this desire in the purest terminology of the Young Germany movement and the philosophy of Ludwig Feuerbach: "What now is the most individual essence of this human nature to which man's longing returns from the farthest distance since it is only here that satisfaction is possible? It is the *necessity of love,* and the essence of this love in its truest expression lies in the *desire for full sensual reality,* for the enjoyment of an object to be grasped with all the senses and firmly and inwardly to be embraced with all the power of one's real existence. In this final and physically certain embrace must not *God* pass away and disappear? Is not the man who longs for God not denied and annihilated?"

It is in fact the Tannhäuser situation once again, but in a surprising reversal. Where Elsa goes wrong is in having brought the "desire for full sensual reality" into her relations with the miracle that is Lohengrin. Only Lohengrin too is guilty in his turn. From the start his mission could not be combined with marriage and with the everyday concerns of a prince. Here, highly personal details of Wagner's inner life are strangely intermingled with his recollections of philosophy and literature: once again the isolation of Wagner the artist in his Saxon surroundings; the triviality of his married and professional life; the ideas of purity and impurity in the literature of the Young German movement; Feuerbach's philosophy of human love which, just as in the case of the Grail and Lohengrin, reinterprets the Christian as the generally human.

In addition, the Lohengrin drama ran its course in Wagner's case against a background of contemporary politics. The patriotic appeals made in the speeches by King Henry (whom Wagner found in his sources) were in the years between 1846 and 1848 understood by Wagner's contemporaries in the sense of the defense of the German homeland against czarism. Richard Wagner thought to make explicit on the stage in *Lohengrin* the contemporary political argument between the spirit of the age and reaction. On this point he expressed himself fairly precisely in an extremely informative letter he wrote later to Franz Liszt on January 30, 1852. It was of course his friendship with Liszt that he had to thank for the first performance of *Lohengrin* at Weimar on August 28, 1850, which happened to be Goethe's birthday: Wagner in exile could not be present to hear his work. Princess Caroline von Sayn-Wittgenstein, Liszt's mistress, had written to Wagner about the Weimar performance and the singer who played Ortrud. Wagner answered: "I was fascinated by her clever remarks about the role of Ortrud and the comparison she drew between the achievements of the former and present performer in the part. Your honored lady friend will at once recognize my own preference as soon as I describe my own view of this character simply by saying that Ortrud is a woman

Franz Liszt, 1856. Lithograph by Kniehuber.

who—*is ignorant of love.* This is the whole terrible truth. Her essence is politics. A political man is repugnant, but a political *woman* makes one shudder, and I had to represent this loathsome quality. There is love in this woman, love for the past, for races that have gone down to extinction, the shockingly insane love of pride of birth that can only express itself as hatred for everything that is alive and really exists. In a man such a love is laughable, but in a woman terrible because woman, given her naturally strong need for love, *must* love something, and pride of birth, proclivity towards the past, thus turns into murderous fanaticism. In history we know no more fearful phenomenon than political women. It is not the fact that she is jealous of Elsa, perhaps over Friedrich, that determines Ortrud, but her entire passion is disclosed only in the scene in the second act where, after Elsa's disappearance from the balcony, she springs up from the steps of the cathedral and calls on her old long-forgotten gods. She is a reactionary, intent only on the old and therefore hostile to everything that is new, and indeed a reactionary in the wildest sense of the word: she would like to destroy the world and nature only to bring her decayed gods back to life. Yet in Ortrud this is no obstinate pathological mood; she accepts this passion with all the furious rage of a woman's need to love, even though in her case this need is merely rudimentary, undeveloped, and lacking an object; and therefore she is terribly *magnificent.*"

But here too Richard Wagner remained in an individual way tied to the ideas of the literature of the Young German movement, even while he fought them. The emancipation or politicization of women, whichever one likes to call it, was a major theme of the Young Germans. With the character of Ortrud the Wagner of 1845 opposed to these ideas the bogy of a woman who has become a political animal, but a woman whose politics are directed to what is obsolete and, in Wagner's sense, reactionary. Five years earlier in his *Judith* Friedrich Hebbel, similarly on his own avowal, had put on the stage the impossibility of a woman involved in politics as a counterthesis to ideas of emancipation.

In composing the music for *Lohengrin* Wagner started at the end. He began setting the third act in the autumn of 1846. By March 1847 the composition of the final act had been completed; this involved establishing each leitmotiv and also working out their contrapuntal combinations for the musical climaxes. Wagner now returned to the beginning and composed the first and then finally the second act. When he wrote to Ferdinand Heine in August the music of the actual opera was ready. It was only then that the prelude was written.

In practice *Lohengrin* for the first time forms a musical unity to an extent that had not yet been experienced on the opera stage. The old principle of separate numbers is now finally given up. The work may be divided into scenes but each act is composed as an undivided whole. The leitmotivs serve first of all to characterize the personages, events on the stage, and the ideas involved. The motivs attached to Lohengrin himself, to God's judgment and to the ban on questions are cast in such a form and presented in such a way both on their first appearance and whenever they recur to underline the significance of the action that they can be sure of the listener's attention. In *Lohengrin* the leitmotiv technique is still of a thoroughly dramatic and operatic kind. It is not yet a case, as in the later works, of leitmotivs being combined in the service of psychological analysis. In fact *Lohengrin* does not yet reach that epic musical style which Thomas Mann had in mind when he described Richard Wagner's music dramas as the German contribution to the art of the novel in the nineteenth century. The individuality of the new musical style, which some years later the composer was to characterize by the concept of "absolute melody," is closely connected with Wagner's estrangement from the predictable rhythms and traditional forms of folk song and folk dance. Once again this new principle of music drama is developed in his *Communication to my Friends*.

Wagner made a conscious sacrifice of the popular style of the ballads, folk songs and choruses of the *Dutchman* and of the arias and the French or Italian cantilenas that were still to be found in the score of *Tannhäuser*. The music of *Lohengrin* renounced totally what was conventionally understood as the popular style. When the music used to depict the character of Lohengrin took on a new, nonpopular and uncompromising style, this style corresponded completely to the central theme of the isolation of the artist from the bustle of everyday life. A music of absolute melody corresponded to the spiritual absolutism of the character of Lohengrin. This in turn meant that what Wagner described as the aura of sound hovering around Lohengrin was distinguished as far as possible from the rhythm and melody of folk song. Lohengrin's own theme, as it appears in enchanting diminution in Elsa's vision, then to emerge in triumphant fortissimo to form the instrumental conclusion to the Grail narration in the basic key of A major, is once again given a very precise individual rhythmic form, but hardly in keeping with the rhythms of popular music. The rest of the music connected with Lohengrin is by contrast notable for its lulling and bewitching effect. Throughout the opera the wealth of harmonic invention takes precedence over rhythmic patterns: the typical harmonic language of the music of *Lohengrin* displays itself less through boldness and audacity than through its summoning up of the magical and the primitive.

The music of Telramund and Ortrud is still much more strongly imprisoned within the romantic operatic style of Weber and Marschner and even of *The Flying Dutchman*. On the other hand Wagner succeeded in deriving a quite individual style of melodic line from the rhythm and intonation of the spoken word, with the result that the music of *Lohengrin,* in conjunction

56

with its renunciation of the contemporary popular language of music, was suddenly able to found a new popular musical language. This is among the great achievements of recent musical history. There is a straight line from the melodic line of *Lohengrin* to the speech-like melodic line Janáček was to write in *Jenufa.*

The prelude to Lohengrin also breaks with all the traditions of the operatic overture, even with those of Wagner's preceding works. No longer is it a case of a musical précis or summary of the action as in the prelude to the *Dutchman.* Nor is it any more a musical invocation of the conflicting ideas as in the *Tannhäuser* overture. The prelude to *Lohengrin* does not offer either a symphonic poem or pure symphonic music: it is neither absolute music nor program music. Rather it provides the building up of a musical picture. To reverse what Beethoven said of his Sixth Symphony, it is scene painting far more than the expression of emotions. This was intentional. In exile, besides other explanations for program notes, Wagner provided an interpretation of the prelude to *Lohengrin* which he later included in the fifth volume of his collected writings. Once again he begins as a loyal pupil of Feuerbach. The reinterpretation of the Grail to signify what is generally human is emphasized: "Love seemed to have disappeared from a world of hatred and strife: in no human community did it show itself any longer clearly as the lawgiver. Out of the desolate anxiety for gain and possession, the sole guide of all human intercourse, the human heart's indestructible demand for love at last longed once again for the fulfillment of a need that, the more ardent and exuberant it grew under the pressure of reality, the less it could be contented in this reality. The enraptured power of imagination therefore set both the source and the outcome of this incomprehensible urge to love outside the real world, and, out of the need for a consoling physical representation of this transcendental reality, gave it a miraculous form, which soon was believed, longed for and sought after as really present though unapproachably distant, under the name of the "holy Grail."

In *Lohengrin* Wagner depicted his own existence and at the same time the existence of art, and not just his own art, in modern society. The complex of problems personified in Lohengrin struck him as unique, highly personal, and untypical. It was not. The theme was the artist and the bourgeois world. The preconditions for romantic art were decaying. Exactly ten years after the completion of *Lohengrin* Flaubert finished telling the story of Madame Bovary. But Emma Bovary belongs alongside Lohengrin. For the two artists concerned with the same subject, Gustave Flaubert and Richard Wagner, the European revolution of 1848/49 meant a turning point. In Wagner's case it was a taking up of Arthur Schopenhauer's doctrines of education; in Flaubert's the story of the passive hero Frédéric Moreau, who similarly had to undergo his *éducation sentimentale* in the course of the 1848 revolution.

REVOLUTION AND REVOLUTIONARY

RICHARD WAGNER lived through this period of German revolutionarly conflict as an artist and as a man involved in politics, who had to try to make the connection between his own special aspirations as an artist and the literary and philosophical insights he had gained from the Young Germany movement and from Feuerbach, Proudhon, and Stirner. Wagner was neither able nor willing to commit himself to a program of revolution without taking into account whether this program was capable of furthering his own musical and theatrical ideas. The revolution was *his* revolution. Certainly for him too it was a question of German unity, of new constitutional forms; but for him it was above all a question of the realization of his artistic projects. Since up to now the Saxon Court and the administration of the Dresden Court Theater had offered very stubborn opposition to the plans for reform put forward by Wagner the royal conductor, Richard Wagner inclined towards republican leanings. Whether he was a monarchist republican or a republican monarchist, he was above all a revolutionary for whom it was a question of reform of art and of the theater. The victory of the revolution was thought of as a victory for the theory and practice of the artist Richard Wagner. This leitmotiv runs through all his revolutionary activities and writings from March 1848 until the first week of May the following year.

Much bitterness had accumulated during the years of conducting in Dresden.

But there had nevertheless been many great achievements. In the repertoire Wagner had consistently had regard for the traditions of German opera. As a conductor and composer he worked as the successor of Carl Maria von Weber and the continuator of his work. A performance of *Euryanthe* was given; Wagner used themes from this opera to compose a piece of funeral music, and he gave a speech at the graveside of the composer of *Der Freischütz.* On Palm Sunday 1846, a demonstration performance of Beethoven's Ninth Symphony was arranged with Wagner as conductor. In 1847 Gluck was included in the newly founded German operatic traditions. As a result of his preoccupation with Gluck, at the same time as he was studying Greek art and philosophy, Wagner revised the score of *Iphigenia in Aulis* and successfully rehearsed this opera.

All this was significant and artistically successful, but it did not seem to be enough. The revival of *Rienzi* was a failure. *Tann-*

Richard Wagner as conductor. Silhouette by W. Bithorn.

häuser was not a success. The possibilities of performing his new opera *Lohengrin* in Dresden did not seem at all good. And Wagner as conductor was perpetually at loggerheads with the management of the opera. In addition he was plainly no longer capable of tolerating other artists alongside him or taking precedence over him, even if they were of the highest quality. Robert Schumann, who was working at the same time in Dresden as a concert conductor and teacher of composition, was secretly an annoyance. Mendelssohn's sudden death on November 4, 1847 removed the occasion for serious conflicts. The autobiography *My Life* shows how Wagner experienced as a painful burden the successes enjoyed by the conductor and composer Mendelssohn-Bartholdy, and Wagner even seems to hint that the feeling was mutual.

In the theater Wagner aimed at sole mastery, and there could be no doubt about this. Karl Gutzkow's appointment to the Saxon Court Theater gave him the opportunity to achieve a close limitation of the playwright's responsibilities. The Young German dramatist was to be excluded from having any influence over the opera and its repertoire. In these conflicts Wagner openly took sides in the literary arguments of the Young German school: he was for Heinrich Laube and against Karl Gutzkow. This led to the first serious quarrels with the Royal Theater Director, Baron von Lüttichau. When the revolution broke out in early 1848, Wagner seemed to see a possibility of finding a legal basis for control over the theatrical life of Dresden. He wrote his *Plan for a National Theater for the Kingdom of Saxony*. The account he himself has given of this episode in *My Life* is contradicted by documents in the Burrell Collection. What is certain is that Wagner submitted his plan to the administration of the Court Theater without, as he himself admits, informing his fellow conductors or the members of the Court Chapel.

Was Richard Wagner a revolutionary? He himself did his best later to play down the importance of the whole proceedings. His participation in the Dresden uprising was represented as an outburst of theatrical enthusiasm on the part of an easily aroused but genuinely unpolitical artist. Thus arose the picture of an artist, conductor of the Royal Saxon Opera, who genuinely without guilt found himself manning the barricades, had to flee, very quickly repented his actions in exile, and finally, despite his open penitence, only received his well-deserved amnesty late and with great difficulty.

In fact this is just not so. The assertions in *My Life* are not tenable. There Wagner presents things as if he, still to begin

61

with very much preoccupied with completing *Lohengrin,* had looked up and blinked to find the revolution had broken out and now started to take a little interest in politics. In *My Life* one reads: "Thanks to my older friend Franck I had indeed already been sufficiently well educated in the making of political judgments, so as to go along with so many others in doubting whether the German parliament that was now assembling would be useful and effective; and yet I could not avoid the influence of the indistinct though confident general mood, the belief that was everywhere becoming apparent, that a return to former conditions was impossible. Only instead of words I wanted deeds, and deeds in fact of a kind that would make our princes break irrevocably with their old tendencies that were such an obstacle to the German commonwealth. With these views I was inspired to write a popular poetic appeal to the German princes and peoples to undertake a great martial effort against Russia, since it was ultimately from there that the pressure seemed to be exercised on German politics with the effect of so fatally alienating the princes from their peoples. One stanza ran:

> It is the old fight against the east
> that returns today:
> the people must not let the sword rust,
> if they want freedom for themselves."

The spirit of these verses is in total correspondence with the corresponding lines given to King Henry and even to Lohengrin in Wagner's opera: the continuity of political thinking is thus plain. No less obvious is the relationship between the manifestos Wagner was now writing as a politician in the course of the revolution and the new artistic plans evolved by the writer and composer after the completion of *Lohengrin.* The fact that in that early summer of 1848 almost the only friend he clung to was the failed musician and passionate revolutionary August

Röckel—to the extent of making common cause with Röckel from now on even on political matters—also belies the thesis of an unpolitical musician sliding into involvement in the revolution. The recollections of Dresden citizens give the impression that later the *bien pensants* saw Röckel as having seduced and corrupted Wagner. Richard Wagner himself was more honorable. He continued to revere the memory of the unusal but important figure of his friend of the revolution.

Through Röckel Richard Wagner, the discontented and debt-laden musician and politician who was keen on reform, came into contact with the life of Dresden's political parties. Wagner joined the Fatherland Association, the gathering place of the left, of the genuine republicans; and it was before them, taking the place of Röckel, who was no orator, that he spoke on the subject "What is the Attitude to the Monarchy of Efforts Towards Republicanism?"

Their attitude to the monarchy was indeed quite singular. Richard Wagner began calling for "the downfall of the last glimmer of aristocratism." The abolition of the aristocratic upper house went without question for the men of the Fatherland Association and also for the conductor Wagner. The same applied to universal suffrage: "Further we want the unconditional right of voting and election to be granted to every adult person born in the country: the poorer he is and the more he is in need of aid, the more natural is his claim to take part in drawing up the laws that are to protect him against poverty and need."

Logically one would now expect a democratic republican program to follow: abolishing the power of the aristocracy ought really to start with the removal of the monarchy. But this was not at all the way Richard Wagner thought. He knew people would raise objections and accuse him of being illogical: "But now you ask me whether I want to achieve all this *with* the monarchy. Not for a moment have I been able to lose sight of its

63

existence—even if you have regarded it as impossible and have pronounced its death sentence. But if you have to recognize it as possible, as I regard it as more than possible, then the republic would embody justice if—and this is the condition we must demand—*the king* should be *the first and most upright of republicans.* And is there anyone who has a greater vocation to be the truest and most loyal republican than the *prince?* Res publica means the business of the people. Which single person can be more determined on that than the prince, whose entire attitudes, thoughts and endeavors appertain solely to the business of the people? What should be able to move him, in the conviction he has gained of his vocation to rule, to diminish himself and to want to belong merely to a particular *smaller* section of the people?"

The conception became ever more adventurous: the republican sang the praises of the House of Wettin. The unhappy demand for a "revolution from above," for a compromise between the princes and the bourgeoisie that since the German Enlightenment had so fatally been canvased in Germany and finally led to the founding of the Empire in 1871, appeared completely intelligible to such an apparently consistent republican as Richard Wagner. His ideas—this medley of republicanism, reform from above, Feuerbach, Stirner and Proudhon—were like an illustration of that which is attacked in the *Communist Manifesto* under the label "true socialism." As a "true socialist" Richard Wagner fought against the "coarsely destructive" communism of Marx and Engels. The Communist Federation derided the standpoint of true socialism, and thus those of Richard Wagner too, as the sultry rigmarole of aesthetes and semi-philosophers.

Whatever one's view may be of Richard Wagner as a revolutionary, he represented a typical attitude: in no way is he an alien element in this curious German revolution. He belonged to it and it belonged to him. There was not for a moment any dichotomy between Richard Wagner the revolutionary and Richard Wagner the artist: lines from the libretto of *Lohengrin* are transformed into poems of political conflict, the thoughts of the political orator and agitator are translated without difficulty into the world of opera and drama. As a writer and composer of operas Richard Wagner was interested in a remarkable project which once again, as with *Lohengrin,* was conceived as a blending of myth and history: a synthesis of Nibelung myth and Hohenstaufen history. Frederick Barbarossa, the Ghibellines and the Nibelungs were the material for what was planned as *The Wibelungs.*

Wagner's revolutionary ideas find their apex in his well-known pamphlet *Revolution.* The socialist utopia had now taken on the form of a rhapsody. The conclusion has the effect of an anticipation of the later Nietzsche—Dionysos or the Crucified. But in the case of Wagner this is not an alternative but a synthesis: "Closer and closer rolls the storm and on its wings the revolution; wide are opened the hearts of those awakened to life and the revolution victoriously invades their brains, their bones, their flesh, and completely fulfills them. In godlike ecstasy they spring up from the earth, no longer are they the poor, the hungry, those bowed down by misery, they carry themselves proudly, enthusiasm radiates from their ennobled faces, a radiant gleam streams from their eyes, and with a cry that shakes heaven: 'I am a man!' the millions, the living revolution, man made God, hurl themselves into the valleys and plains and proclaim to the whole world the new gospel of happiness."

The extent to which this way of thinking remained shut in on itself and was able to go on working in the first period of exile despite the defeat of the revolutionary is shown by the first great manifesto of Wagner in exile—*Art and Revolution.* This—in agreement throughout with his specifically revolutionary writings —reached its climax in a synthesis of Jesus and Apollo.

65

Chaotic and consistent: these adjectives describe the thoughts, speeches and pamphlets of this revolutionary during this revolution. Chaotic and yet consistent also describe his practical activity between March 1848 and the May uprising of 1849. Wagner's speeches at the Fatherland Association on monarchy and republican efforts had naturally ruined his name with the Court, at the theater, and with the entire conservative bourgeoisie of Dresden. In the press he was derided as "Dr. Richard Faust."

Wagner now went on journeys: to Vienna, where he experienced the effects and the deceptive euphoria of the March revolutions; to Weimar, where he sought out Liszt at the Crown Prince Hotel and came to a closer human and artistic relationship. Then he returned to Dresden. August Röckel, who had temporarily been arrested, was zealously active as a journalist and socialist agitator. Richard Wagner continued to stand by him. Both belonged to the most radical wing of the Saxon revolutionaries. Wagner adopted Röckel's Proudhonism completely and enthusiastically. There were only two of Röckel's ideas he was unwilling to accept: the abolition of marriage and the equality of all working people without any special system for artists. Wagner was to state this candidly later in his autobiography. In actual fact what was involved here was no longer an abstract idea about humanity, no longer art and human society, but an intellectual consequence that Richard Wagner was in no way willing to accept as an artist and as a man. There could be no equality without an exception made for him.

As far as Wagner was concerned the ideas of the Young German movement were linked with the person of Heinrich Laube; Feuerbach and Proudhon he knew from their books; now he entered upon a new and decisive acquaintance that was to have an extraordinary influence on him both as a person and with regard to his ideas.

Michail Alexandrovich Bakunin, born in 1814 and thus al-

Michail Bakunin (1814–1876). Engraving by W. Barbotin.

most exactly Wagner's contemporary, had left property, title, and
commission behind in Russia in order to devote himself to the
revolutionary cause in western and central Europe. Between 1840
and 1849 he was to be found wherever anything was afoot in
Europe. When the elderly Schelling, appointed by Frederick
William IV to the chair left vacant by Hegel, gave his lectures on
the philosophy of revelation in the winter semester of 1841/42,
Bakunin was in the lecture theater along with Sören Kierkegaard,
Jacob Burckhardt, and Friedrich Engels. When a year later, in
the autumn of 1842, Georg Herwegh progressed through Ger-
many as a celebrated revolutionary poet, he was accompanied by
Bakunin. Then he lived as a political exile in Switzerland, in
Brussels, in Paris. He took part in the February revolution. When

Georg Herwegh (1817–1875). Engraving by Gonzenbach after a painting by Hitz.

preparations were being made in Germany for the elections to the national assembly at Frankfurt and the different German Fatherland Associations had organized a general conference at Leipzig, naturally Bakunin turned up too—straight from Paris.

It was almost unavoidable that this man, who traveled on to Dresden to live there under the assumed name of Dr. Schwartz, should have had a very strong effect on Richard Wagner. Bakunin was the essence of a revolutionary; and in addition a mortal enemy of czars and czarism. To him the revolution seemed equivalent to the Russian revolution. Now the circle was formed. Bakunin was a friend of Georg Herwegh, Herwegh recommended him to August Röckel, Röckel brought Bakunin and

Wagner together, and a few years later Wagner was to be Herwegh's companion in exile in Zurich. And while Herwegh in this way introduced the revolutionary Michail Bakunin to the revolutionary Richard Wagner, five years later in Zurich he was to introduce Wagner to something with highly important consequences for him as an artist and thinker: Schopenhauer's book *The World as Will and Idea*.

Practical activity, choice of friends, and theoretical convictions had all come together. Early in the morning of May 4, 1849, armed revolt broke out in Dresden. The demand was for the implementation of the imperial constitution drawn up at Frank-

The revolution in Dresden. The storming of the Rome Hotel and assault on the barricades, May, 1849.

furt. The government of the Kingdom of Saxony countered that the Frankfurt constitution had lapsed because Frederick William IV of Prussia had refused the proffered imperial crown. The King of Saxony formed a new government hostile to the revolution and called on Prussian troops for help to prevent the violent implementation of the Frankfurt constitution by the democratic and republican party. On May 3 barricades were built, on May 4 the court and the government fled to the fortress of Königstein, whereupon a provisional government was formed in Dresden itself. Up to May 5 a truce was maintained, but meanwhile the Prussian troops had arrived. The Dresden revolutionaries on the other hand received almost no reinforcements. Their sympathizers in Leipzig made inflammatory speeches but did not prevent the Saxon garrison from withdrawing and moving against Dresden on the orders of the royal government. Street fighting began on the afternoon of May 6. Involved were Prussian artillery, two battalions of Prussian infantry, and the Saxon regiments as well. The cavalry cut the reinforcements off, the barricades were bombarded by the artillery. Michail Bakunin, the former officer of the czar's army, was in practice the only one in command on the barricades. The image of this man with his "enormous beard" imprinted itself strongly on the minds of the survivors. The troops loyal to the government forced their way into the inner city on May 7. Richard Wagner's place of work, the old opera house, went up in flames. On the evening of May 8 the leaders of the provisional government and of the revolt decided to withdraw with their fighters to the Erzgebirge, the range of mountains some twenty to twenty-five miles south of the city, in order to continue the struggle from Freiberg, a town twenty miles southwest of Dresden.

The artists of the Fatherland Association were on the side of the revolt. August Röckel was a soldier and officer; Gottfried Semper, the architect, built barricades which were found to offer remarkable resistance to the enemy. Richard Wagner had dis-

70

tributed manifestos and found himself under fire. On May 7 he was manning an observation post in the tower of the Holy Cross church.

On May 9 he too, "united with Minna in a one-horse carriage," withdrew to the Erzgebirge. In Freiberg he joined up with Bakunin. Meanwhile the provisional government had discovered that the Freiberg authorities were not ready to join with the rebels in continuing the struggle. It was decided to move on to Chemnitz (now Karl-Marx-Stadt), twenty miles further on. Bakunin hurried on ahead. Wagner followed on later to arrive in Chemnitz late at night. That was his good luck, since Bakunin and the other revolutionaries had already been arrested. The Chemnitz authorities were loyal to the king and had overcome the rebels in order to hand them over to the government. Wagner, who had not been discovered, thus succeeded in fleeing. He first of all reached Weimar.

Meanwhile Bakunin and August Röckel had been captured. The Russian faced extradition to the autocrat of all the Russians. Röckel was sentenced to death, but this was commuted to penal servitude for life. He spent eleven years in the prison at Waldheim. One hundred and seventy-eight rebels were killed in Dresden. The government troop losses were officially given as 34 dead and 36 wounded.

The following warrant was issued for the arrest of Richard Wagner:

The Royal conductor Richard Wagner of this city, described more fully below, is wanted for investigation on account of material participation in the movement of revolt that took place in this city, but has not yet been reached. The attention of all police authorities is therefore drawn to this man; they are requested to arrest Wagner if he should be found and to inform us of the fact as soon as possible.

Dresden, May 16, 1849.   For the City Police Deputation
                                                    (signed) von Oppell.

Wagner is 37–38 years old, of medium height, has brown hair and wears spectacles.

71

Steckbrief.

Der unten etwas näher bezeichnete Königl. Capellmeister

Richard Wagner von hier ist wegen wesentlicher Theilnahme an der in hiesiger Stadt stattgefundenen aufrührerischen Bewegung zur Untersuchung zu ziehen, zur Zeit aber nicht zu erlangen gewesen. Es werden daher alle Polizeibehörden auf denselben aufmerksam gemacht und ersucht, Wagnern im Betretungsfalle zu verhaften und davon uns schleunigst Nachricht zu ertheilen.

Dresden, den 16. Mai 1849.

Die Stadt-Polizei-Deputation.

von Oppell.

Wagner ist 37—38 Jahre alt, mittler Statur, hat braunes Haar und trägt eine Brille.

Steckbrief.

The warrant for Wagner's arrest.

On May 22 the outlaw made a six-hour trek to reach Jena, where he met Minna in the house of the Jena professor Wolff. Liszt had given him money and the advice to make for France to work there as a conductor and opera composer. But since it was inadvisable to go through Prussian territory Wagner chose to go through Switzerland. Another Jena professor, Widmann, gave him his passport. By way of Rudolstadt, Coburg, and Lichtenfels Wagner reached Lindau, crossed Lake Constance, and landed on Swiss soil on the morning of May 28, 1849, at Rorschach. Eduard Devrient received a letter in the refugee's handwriting, to be forwarded to Minna. Bakunin and Röckel were behind bars, Gottfried Semper too found himself fleeing to Switzerland. The revolution was over. The revolutionary was an exile. But he was in safety.

OPERA AND DRAMA

FOR the refugee Wagner, Switzerland was originally merely a country to pass through; in Weimar Franz Liszt had advised him to try his luck once again in Paris. Wagner therefore set out and attempted for the second time to win the French capital for himself and his new art. Disillusion was unavoidable. The revolution was over in France too. The world of the financiers emerged unscathed from the crisis, and with them were now associated the *industriels* who were continually becoming more powerful. But their artistic tastes also ran to grand opera, as in the days of the bourgeois monarchy.

For Wagner hardly anything had changed in Paris and in its artistic life since his years of poverty there. He was forced to recognize this very soon. Liszt sent him three hundred francs so that the exile could return to Switzerland. The balance was drawn in an embittered letter written to Ferdinand Heine on November 18, 1849: "Eight days in Paris were enough to enlighten me about the violent error I had fallen into. Allow me here to let off steam to you about the shocking worthlessness of artistic activity in Paris, in other words the opera. Over the last few decades the artistic affairs of the Paris opera have become under Meyerbeer's financial influence so stinkingly horrible that an honorable person can have nothing to do with them. Although Liszt's secretary Belloni—an extremely clever and very good-natured person who knows the lie of the land—had, luckily for me, taken an interest in the business, although he had introduced me to a poet, Gustav Vaes (at present president of the *Commission d'auteurs*), who was waiting for the outline of a libretto from me so as to

73

deliver the book at once and to bring about its acceptance on my behalf by the directors of the Grand Opera, yet I am most firmly convinced that never ever will I succeed in really bringing about the performance of an opera of mine at the Academy, at least not under present conditions and given the spirit predominant *now* and the *present* régime. As things are at present, Meyerbeer has everything in his hand, or rather in his purse; and the marsh of intrigue one has to wade through is too great, so that quite different and more artful people like myself have long since given up the idea of engaging in a battle in which money is the only thing that decides matters."

He now decided to settle by the lake of Zurich. Minna was brought along to set up a new household. Old and new friends provided further help. The situation of his first stay in Paris was repeated in his artistic life: as then, the humiliated refugee, lacking any position or firm income, felt himself inclined to write and capable of doing so, but neither inclined nor able to compose operas. The remainder of 1849 and the whole of 1850 thus provide a certain high point in Wagner's cultural and philosophical writings, while the dramatic subjects stagnated.

Three theoretical writings attempted to draw the balance of his artistic experiences to date. The essay on *Art and the Revolution* (1849) is in its character a pamphlet that really belongs to the range of revolutionary pamphlets. Then there followed, in book form and published by Wigand of Leipzig, *The Work of Art of the Future* (1850). In the same year Wagner wrote an essay on *Art and Climate* but devoted his chief strength to the most comprehensive and ambitious of his books on culture and the theory of art: *Opera and Drama.* The foreword is dated Zurich, January 1851. The book appeared in three volumes a year later. In addition Wagner could not forego a fresh attempt—his third —at the artistic conquest of the French capital. All judgments in the theoretical writings that were coming to maturity at this

74

Minna Wagner.

time must therefore be read against the background of such a venture.

A love affair provided a further incitement to this third journey to France. Jessie Taylor, a young Englishwoman who was very musical, had already visited him in Dresden. Now she told him she was living in Bordeaux as Madame Laussot. Eugène Laussot was very well off and was also ready to meet Jessie's wish to bring the German composer to the Garonne, even though he appeared not to have very much understanding for the artistic leanings of his wife. Wagner arrived in Bordeaux, after he had tried in vain in Paris to sell the barely sketched out libretto for *Wieland the Smith* just as he had succeeded in doing with the libretto of the *Dutchman.* There now arose between Richard Wagner and Jessie Laussot a remarkable love story that had all the accents of genuine passion and yet in its course lacked stability and seriousness, so that it concluded in banal compromise.

Wagner had come to the decision to flee with Jessie to Greece and Asia Minor. But now the antagonists stepped on the stage: Minna Wagner and Eugène Laussot. Lacking, however, were the pathetic element of Fricka and the tragic element of King Mark. The lovers gave in without a real struggle. When Minna turned up in Paris, Richard Wagner retreated to the shores of Lake Geneva. In *My Life* he described his last visit to Bordeaux quite graphically. But the documents in the Burrell Collection contain very touching letters from Minna and also a very dignified letter from Ann Taylor, Jessie's mother.

In May 1850 he celebrated his thirty-seventh birthday at Villeneuve with Julie Ritter and her son Karl, then returned to his home in Zurich. In Germany the opera composer Richard Wagner now first began to win general fame, above all after the success of the first performance in Weimar of *Lohengrin* and chiefly thanks to Liszt's energetic attempts at publicity. In May 1853, to mark his fortieth birthday, he was able to organize the first Wagner festival at the Zurich City Theater. There was a public reading of the foreword to the three libretti of the *Dutchman, Tannhäuser,* and *Lohengrin,* and substantial extracts from these works were then given concert performances over the three days of the festival. It was the first time Wagner had been able to conduct extracts from the music of *Lohengrin* himself. Zurich also provided the first example of what later was to become the rule and, after the founding of Bayreuth, an institution:

Richard Wagner. Lithograph by Hanfstaengel after a painting by Clem-
entine Stocker-Escher, 1853.

singers and instrumentalists came flocking from all parts of
Germany to place themselves at the service of this sole and
unique art.

The year 1852 was spent on journeys inside Switzerland. Wagner traveled through the Bernese Oberland in spring and experienced the rocky landscapes that were to be transformed into the
scenery of *Rhinegold* and the landscape of the second act of
The Valkyrie. He reached Ticino, arrived at Lugano and from
there Lake Maggiore. Here he saw the Borromean Islands, the
landscape of Jean Paul's *Titan.* Since Wagner had to share and
communicate all his impressions, he had Minna and also his
friend and fellow exile in Zurich Georg Herwegh join him.

The libretto of *The Ring of the Nibelung* was completed in the autumn of 1852. From now on it was the composer who had to work. Wagner seemed to look back almost with impatience to the preceding years when he had sacrificed all his energies to theoretical speculation. When in the summer of 1853 Liszt tried to win him over to a joint plan for a periodical, Wagner turned the plan down angrily—although he had just written two theoretical books and several essays as well as a second autobiographical sketch.

Despite all its disorder and its numerous deviations, Richard Wagner's life still continues to appear as an astonishing and organic unity. In retrospect the profusion of theoretical and often rather turgid prose would appear to be just as much a necessity as the later angry rejection of all theorizing for the sake of the new work that had flared up. Wagner was secretly well aware that this new work could not have been possible without the preceding theoretical speculation. In addition it was not just a case of the composer Richard Wagner speculating on the relationship of opera and drama and the art of the future and the present. The three theoretical writings were at the same time planned as a confrontation between Richard Wagner the revolutionary and his historical political experiences. All three pieces are dominated by the leitmotiv that supplies the title of the first of them: art and the revolution. Political experience, humanist philosophy and unfulfilled artistic longings fit together to form a unity. Everything was blended to provide the substance of the *Ring* cycle. And it all left its traces on that work: in the verse, in its meaning, in the music.

Common to the three writings on the theory of art was the fact that Wagner started from the contrast between modern art and that of Greece. This was a typical theme of the enlightenment in Europe. The English social theorists like the French had enquired into the causes of the downfall of ancient civilization, and in particular of the Roman world. German thinking from the time of Winckelmann and Lessing circled around the synthesis of German and Greek, of ancient and modern. Richard Wagner thus remained completely within the traditions of German aesthetics and European revolutionary theory when he thought to construct his essay on *Art and the Revolution* on this contrast of ancient and modern, of the Greek world and modern civilization.

As a pupil of Feuerbach Wagner continued to be an opponent of the link between art and Christianity. Indeed, for him the Christian world was in principle unartistic. But the failed revolutionary noticed a greater enemy of art in modern industry. In this essay Wagner remained as he was, both a democrat and a socialist. It was only on the basis of a renewal of the audience from new sections of the people, from the working classes, whom he wanted to bring into the theater, that he was able to conceive a renaissance of art and its liberation from the rule of Mercury. He was explicitly on the side of the Paris proletariat—and he used this term "proletariat"—in the revolt that failed of June 1848. In Wagner's view the revolution was to liberate men from the constraint of industrial society; art was to disclose a new beauty to them and educate them to become a finer humanity. Once again, as so often with Wagner, it is a synthesis of "true socialism" and classical German humanism.

Wagner however believed in a renewal of society and of art that would no longer "follow money," no longer stand under the sign of Mercury, but have the effect of a synthesis of Jesus and Apollo: "Jesus who suffered for mankind, and Apollo who raised mankind to joyful dignity."

What the philosopher of art and social theorist had proclaimed here for the first time in the form of a thesis he sought to demonstrate in greater detail in his book on *The Work of Art of the Future*. In this new book Wagner himself quite explicitly under-

Ludwig Feuerbach (1804–1872).

lined something that had already become apparent in his essay on the relationship between art and revolution, and particularly in his visions of a new human beauty and emancipation: the powerful imprint of the philosophy of Ludwig Feuerbach. *The Work of Art of the Future* is in fact "dedicated to Ludwig Feuerbach in respectful gratitude." Here too one external detail betrays the profound change that Wagner, both the artist and the revolutionary, was to undergo over the next decades: the book was later to appear without the dedication to Feuerbach.

The conclusion of *The Work of Art of the Future* linked the planned music drama *Wieland the Smith* with trains of thought about art and revolution. The outline of *Wieland* had once again, as previously in *Tannhäuser,* confronted the German and French worlds with each other. French financial domination and the strength of the German people were opposed to each other.

Already we are in the closest neighborhood of the material for the *Ring*. In this hour of greatest need Wieland forges wings for himself that bear him despite his lameness out of the power of Neiding to freedom. The ideas of this *Wieland* sketch are chosen by Wagner to provide the crown for his new book. His essay on art and revolution had for him found its climax in the symbolic blending together of Jesus and Apollo. And by placing the Wieland myth at the conclusion of his ideas about the art of the future Wagner was once again linking art and revolution.

The essay on art and revolution was a preliminary sketch for the book on the work of art of the future. But this book in its turn has the effect of a preliminary sketch when placed against Wagner's giant essay *Opera and Drama.* As with all the writings of this remarkable man it makes a divided impression. What is extremely true and what is extremely false are intertwined with each other, the highest degree of expert knowledge is found side by side with embarrassing examples of unassimilated borrowing of other people's ideas; insights well worth consideration stand side by side with the effects of resentment or of that malignity that eighty years later was to prove extremely pernicious in Germany.

The antithesis of opera and drama which gives the book its title and the basic idea is worked out under four headings. Looking back to the theses he had put forward about the work of art of the future, Wagner contrasts the unfree art of the present with the yet to be liberated art of a future era, of a revolutionary transformation. This antithesis comes from Wagner the socialist. The second antithesis is supplied by Feuerbach but is reinterpreted by Wagner for his own use. Two forms of love are opposed to each other in a setting similar to that of *Tannhäuser:* prostitution and coquetry as against genuine love, or rather human love. The third antithesis is connected with Wagner's patriotic feelings, but also, as always with this artist, with his nationalism. French and Italian art are opposed to a German art. But nevertheless all three antitheses—the revolutionary, the national, the opposition of different kinds of feelings of sympathy —reach their climax in what for the writer is the only substantial antithesis, that between opera and music drama.

In the existing state of the art the drama was merely a means for the development, the unleashing of musical splendor; Wagner wanted to place music at the service of a new musical dramatic art. This led him to diffuse and in places rather worthless considerations about the development of the whole universe of dramatic literature. In a willful genealogy Lessing, Schiller, and Goethe were given the role of precursors: their partial solutions would now be followed by the real final solution which at the same time was the dissolution of all preceding forms. In this context Wagner had a very striking starting point which is not worth discussing as a historical analysis but which as an artist's recognition of his age in the middle of the nineteenth century is very ingenious: "Modern drama has a noble origin: a natural origin, proper to our historical development, the novel; and an alien origin, grafted on to our development through reflection, the Greek drama conceived according to the misunderstood rules of Aristotle.

"The real core of our poetry lies in the novel; in their efforts to make this core as palatable as possible our writers have repeatedly hit upon the more or less close imitation of the Greek drama. The finest flowers of the drama that has its immediate origin in the novel we have in the plays of Shakespeare; at the farthest distance from this drama we encounter its complete contrary in the tragedies of Racine. It is between these two poles that the whole of the rest of our dramatic literature hovers to and fro undecided and uncertain."

Wagner's book ends with an appeal, with a prospect. Myth is no longer taken from past cultures: it offers itself in the future form of the utopia. Strictly speaking it is no longer a question of the work of art of the future but of its creator. The people as the necessary force for the work of art appears to be forced back into the static role reminiscent of the way it appears on the stage in *Rienzi* and *Lohengrin* and later on the festival meadow of the last act of *The Mastersingers. Opera and Drama* is still the work of a revolutionary. It is still living in Feuerbach's utopia; only once again it betrays Lohengrin's isolation. Utopia and renunciation: the new art of the music novel stands under the sign of human love, but it is already talking of the renunciation of love, of the curse of love.

SCHOPENHAUER AS EDUCATOR

LIKE so many of his counterparts, Wagner too, the failed revolutionary, found Arthur Schopenhauer's empire of thought on the road before him. In a letter about Liszt's essay on the *Dutchman* the references to Schopenhauer are still hidden, understandable only to the expert. In the autumn of 1854 there followed, once again in a letter to Liszt, this generous and genuine acknowledgement:

Dear Franz,
   I am continually discovering that you are actually a great philosopher, while I am a real bumpkin. Besides the—slow—progress of my music I have now been exclusively occupying myself with a person who, if only on paper, has entered my isolation like a gift from heaven. It is Arthur Schopenhauer, the greatest philosopher since Kant, whose thoughts he, as he states, was the first to think through completely to the end. For forty years the German professors have—prudently—ignored him; recently however, to Germany's humiliation, he has been discovered by an English critic. Compared with him what charlatans all these Hegels are! His main

Arthur Schopenhauer (1788–1860). Drawing by L. Kleemann.

idea, the final denial of the will to life, is of a fearful seriousness, but simply liberating. Naturally this did not come as something new to me, and no one can have this idea if it is not already living in him. But this philosopher was the first to awaken this idea to this clarity in me. When I think back on the storms of my heart, the fearful convulsions with which—against its will—it clung to hope in life, indeed, when these storms still today often swell up into a hurricane, then against this I have now found a sedative that at last simply helps me to gain sleep during the wakeful night; it is the longing for death planted deep inside man's heart; complete unconsciousness, total nothingness, the disappearance of all dreams —the most unique and final redemption.

Now I have often rediscovered how wonderful your ideas are: you may express them differently, because you are religious, but all the same I know that your meaning is precisely the same. How deep you are! What you said in your essay on the *Dutchman* often struck me with the force of lightning. When I read Schopenhauer, I was for the most part in your company: only you did not notice it. So I am continually becoming more mature: it is only as a way of passing the time that I am still playing with art.

84

Wagner was always concerned to communicate his new impressions and insights to his friends and to those close to him. What he himself had experienced or thought out was to become for them a valid law. Here it was Schopenhauer, who then a few years later, to the annoyance of Minna, was to become the inexhaustible raw material for conversation among the circle of friends on the green hill of the Wesendonk villa. Wagner wanted to convert Liszt too to Schopenhauer, but realized a little awkwardly that the Catholic Christianity of his friend could only with difficulty be joined together with the so completely un-Christian world of Schopenhauer. So in his letter he turned the Catholic Franz Liszt into a Schopenhauerian *malgré lui.*

It is of course not the case that Wagner had been a Schopenhauerian all along without knowing it. That applies neither to Wagner himself nor to Franz Liszt. A great deal had to come together, personal as well as social experiences, in order that Richard Wagner the follower of Feuerbach and Proudhon, the unique pupil of the literature of the Young German movement, could become a disciple of Arthur Schopenhauer.

The remarkably powerful delayed-action effect of a philosophy that emerged from more than thirty years' anonymity and for decades was to become the intellectual experience of young generations of Germans, stretching from Wotan and Parsifal by way of Nietzsche's *Unfashionable Observations* to the world of Thomas Buddenbrooks, is only to be explained by the historical context. Historical activism changed into negation and renunciation of the world. In the eyes of the Young German school and not the least in the eyes of Ludwig Feuerbach, the different forms of love were recognized as the basis of all morality. This emerges in the Young German writers as the conflict between physical and spiritual love, between asceticism and the Greek spirit, and in Feuerbach as the ethic of human love. To this Schopenhauer opposed a totally new system of categories. The fourth book of

85

his major work is concluded by paragraph 66 with its thesis: "All love is compassion." The next section expounds this thesis from its corollary: "And every love that is not compassion is selfishness."

Richard Wagner, around 1855.

This ethical reinterpretation became extremely important for Wagner's art. It did not matter that Schopenhauer had virtually already been applied in his early work. Up to *Lohengrin*—and beyond this in the sketching out of *Jesus* or *Siegfried*—Wagner's art was marked by the affirmation of the will, changing the world, the ethic of love.' These basic standpoints that were in inseparable harmony with the Wagnerian creative genius—Schopenhauer was a thinker, albeit a very musical one, not a creative artist—showed themselves to be so firmly disposed that they could not be completely shaken even by the new experience of Schopenhauer. Hence the new works, from *Tristan* to *Parsifal*, present themselves as temples to Schopenhauer that to a considerable extent have been built from the stones of Wagner's previous shrines—just as the Emperor Justinian fetched the pillars of the temple of Diana of the Ephesians to Constantinople to use them in the building of Hagia Sophia. The internal inconsistency of the *Ring* can offer remarkably strong evidence on this point.

The doctrines of Schopenhauer thus found their fruitful historical moment after the failure of the European revolution. It is moving and deeply symbolic when on February 4, 1855 Richard Wagner writes from Zurich to the publisher in Leipzig of the *Neue Zeitschrift für Musik* to ask him to send a copy of the second edition of *The World as Will and Idea*, just published by Brockhaus, to August Röckel in the prison at Waldheim.

ON THE GREEN HILL

MARCH of 1848, the year of revolution, saw the completion of the composition of *Lohengrin*. In November 1853 Wagner began setting the libretto of *The Rhinegold* to music and in an unparalleled burst of concentration completed the composition in three months. This indicated a flow of musical powers that had long been dammed up. Five and a half years of his life had been spent as an agitator for himself and for the revolution; as an orator and journalist; as a philosopher of culture and dramatist; as a conductor of his own and especially of other people's works. Now at last, from out of this stream of different figures and different activities, the real character of the artist emerged, that of the composer.

Richard Wagner had completed the fortieth year of his life. He resided at Zurich, continually plagued by financial worries, but all the same leading a very comfortable existence. In Germany, France, and England there emerged obvious signs of his growing fame. A group of people had formed in Zurich from German revolutionary exiles and distinguished and well-to-do Swiss citizens, and to this group Richard Wagner belonged, even though he could not yet be regarded as the exclusive focus of these social occasions. Nevertheless in the memoirs she was to publish much later, in 1896, Mathilde Wesendonk saw the Zurich group of that time as a chorus of stars that circled around Wagner as the sun. This was how it appeared to her: "He was a great lover of nature. In his garden he spied out the sparrows' nests, a rose on his desk could make him happy, and the forest murmurs in *Siegfried* tell of the whispering of the lofty tree-tops of the Sihltal forest, whither he directed his steps on long walks, very often in the company of the poet Georg Herwegh. On these occasions the conversation of this pair turned on the philosophy of Arthur Schopenhauer.

"His 'aides-de-camp' were from time to time Tausig and Hans von Bülow. Wagner called Hans his alter ego. Von Bülow's gratitude, unselfishness and self-sacrifice knew no bounds. But Tausig too was touching in his concern to follow the master's wishes to a T. Thus when he was staying in the Wagners' villa as a guest he played dominoes after lunch with Wagner's sickly and excited wife so as not to disturb Wagner's post-prandial nap.

"Gottfried Semper's appointment to the Polytechnic in Zurich was the happiest of events; Gottfried Keller's *Green Henry* and *The People of Seldwyla* were books Wagner would read aloud with consummate mastery. *Mirror, the Kitten, The Three Just Comb-Makers,* and *A Village Romeo and Juliet* were favorites of his.

"Everything that moved him deeply as an artist and as a man he discussed with Frau Eliza Wille at Mariafeld.

"Lastly I must mention the loyalest of the loyal, his family friend Dr. Jacob Sulzer, who also favored Gottfried Keller's reappointment to the cantonal Grand Council and finally brought this about.

"There was no lack of visits from Weimar. Countess d'Agoult did not disdain to travel from Paris to Zurich *pour faire connaissance des grands hommes.*"

Fortunately we possess another description of this group and of its way of life. In a letter of January 13, 1856 Gottfried Keller wrote to Lisa Duncker: "Here in Zurich things are going well for me to date; I enjoy the best company to see all sorts of people of the kind that in Berlin aren't to be found so pleasantly under the same roof. A family from the Rhineland called Wesendonk is here too. Originally they came from Dusseldorf but for some time were in New York. The wife is a very pretty woman née Mathilde Luckemeier, and the couple run an elegant home and are building a magnificent villa on the outskirts of the city; they have taken me to them in a friendly way. Then there are excellent supper parties given by an elegant government councilor at which Richard Wagner, Semper, who built the Dresden theater and museum, Vischer from Tübingen, and several Zurich people meet together, and at which after feasting plentifully one gets a hot cup of tea and a Havana cigar at two

Gottfried Keller (1818–1890). Photograph, 1863.

in the morning. Wagner himself sometimes provides a solid lunch at which there is hearty boozing, so that I who believed myself to be out of the materialism of Berlin have landed out of the frying pan into the fire. I have also already been to various Zurich banquets; the cuisine is very good here, and there is no lack of refinements, so it was high time I came home to preach morality and moderation to my fellow-countrymen; and to this end I must first savor everything carefully to the full so as properly to get to know what I mean to attack."

This group was important and was drawn from several classes of society, but in no way was it yet any kind of Wagner Society. The intellectual leanings of the group were significant. Gottfried Keller and Friedrich Theodor Vischer were close to a view of literature that, as had been the case in *Opera and Drama,* valued the novel, and the epic work of art in general, as the highest art form. This external similarity between Vischer and Wagner went further. Vischer, who taught from 1855 on as professor of aesthetics at the University of Zurich and the Technical Institute, was also now completing a reexamination of his aesthetic principles in the light of his experiences of the revolution.

In this context of intellectual debate that was to be representative for the intellectual life of the German bourgeoisie during the rest of the century, Gottfried Keller was the one who remained both moderate and consistent. Even during his days in Berlin and Heidelberg Keller had never been as committed to revolutionary action as Wagner or Herwegh. He had never taken seriously the Young Hegelians' theories of egoism, and thus did not need to reinterpret Max Stirner's anarchistic egoism in a religious sense as Vischer was later to do: in 1873, Vischer when Wagner too has started on the turn toward religion, Vischer was to write, "Religion is the thawing of egoism." On the other hand, Feuerbach's philosophy had become a liberating experience for Keller too, as the first version of *Green Henry* amply demonstrates. But in contrast to Wagner, Vischer, and Herwegh, Keller was the only one who did not make the transition from Feuerbach to Schopenhauer. His account of the social life of Wagner's circle thus provides a happy contrast.

The years in Zurich from 1853 to 1858 were to an extraordinary extent significant for the history of German culture. Even without Richard Wagner there was an important system of intellectual coordinates. But it was in Wagner's creation that the development of extraordinary potential was consummated. The libretto of the *Ring* was completed. The music of *The Rhinegold* was composed from November 1853 to January 1854. This new year saw the genesis of the music for *The Valkyrie*. The next year, 1855, found Richard Wagner conducting eight large-scale concerts for the London Philharmonic Society in England. The autumn served for work on the score of *The Valkyrie* and its orchestration. The first and second acts of *Siegfried* originated between September 1856 and July 1857. To this was now added *Tristan*—the writing of the libretto and the beginning of composing the music. To the same epoch belong *Five Poems by an Amateur Set to Music for Woman's Voice, by Richard Wagner:* the *Wesendonk-Lieder,* poems by Mathilde Wesendonk which Wagner set, in two cases treating them as sketches for the future music of *Tristan.*

Until they moved to the "refuge" on the green hill next door to the Wesendonk villa, Richard and Minna Wagner lived in one of the Escher houses on the Zeltweg. The house where *The Rhinegold, The Valkyrie* and the first part of *Siegfried* were written is still standing today. The Zurich theater and opera house are not far from where Wagner was living then. Also in the neighborhood are the house where Gottfried Keller was born and the house where Georg Büchner died. In the 1850's the Escher houses on the Zeltweg formed part of the suburbs of Zurich, close to the city center proper but enjoying a certain isolation.

As always in Wagner's life, these years too saw many journeys, visits, stays at spas, and convalescent trips. Wagner visited Paris once again, and there for the first time, on October 10, 1853, he met Liszt's daughter Cosima, then a girl of sixteen. The London concerts meant a great deal of trouble but were also a great success. There were friendships old and new: Berlioz, Hans von Bülow, the pianists Karl Tausig and Karl Klindworth, Malwida von Meysenburg. Wagner learned from the harmonic language of Franz Liszt's new symphonic poems and from great B minor Piano Sonata by Liszt, which Klindworth played to him in London. He received money from Liszt, from Otto Wesendonk, from giving concerts. His home on the Zeltweg was very richly furnished. Wagner worked like one possessed and was fundamentally not willing to divert his energies in any normal vocation.

The Wesendonk villa and the "refuge," Zurich.

In April 1857 he was offered a refuge on the green hill, far from the city and its noise and the smith's hammering. Nor did it involve any substantial expenditure. It was offered him by Otto Wesendonk on a lease for life at a yearly rent of 800 francs. The grounds of the Wesendonk villa are still lovely. But the former Enge outside the city has long since been included within the Zurich city boundaries. It even has its own railway station, Zurich-Enge, on the line leading out to the right bank of the lake. Not far away is Kilchberg, where Conrad Ferdinand Mayer and Thomas Mann lived and are buried. Yet, even though it has long been drawn into the city, the Wesendonk villa on the green hill has a remarkably anachronistic effect. Indeed it undoubtedly had such an effect at the time when Otto Wesendonk had this pretentious building constructed in an imitation of the Renaissance style.

Otto and Mathilde Wesendonk were not Swiss but came from

the Rhineland. Both originated from Elberfeld. Otto was born in 1815, Mathilde Luckemeyer in 1828. Otto was a partner in a New York silk firm whose sole representative he was in Germany. Mathilde Luckemeyer also came from a rich commercial family, the daughter of a commercial councilor in the service of the Kingdom of Prussia. She married Otto Wesendonk in 1848, when she was nineteen. A first son died a few months after the birth. But from 1851 onwards she bore three children, a daughter and two sons. Her second son, Karl Wesendonk, was born in April 1857, around the time Otto Wesendonk offered his friend Richard Wagner the neighboring small house on the green hill. Mathilde Wesendonk was very gifted, musical, responsive to poetry of the late romantic tradition, as can be seen from the poems of hers that Wagner set. She was cultivated and fastidious, but basically hard and decisive when it came to the carrying out of what she wanted. If one reads her later reminiscences of Wagner in order to compare them with the artist's own letters and diary entries, it looks as if Mathilde Wesendonk was the stronger driving force. Here too, as in the more successful "recapitulation" that was to follow later, Wagner is as it were an object of domination.

The Wesendonk marriage was obviously happy. Otto Wesendonk was magnanimous, cultured, sympathetic. He behaved very well during the later conflict: he, who was barely two years younger than Richard Wagner, showed during the crisis something of the dignity of King Mark. The marriage between Richard and Minna had long since broken down. Minna, who suffered severely from heart trouble, had to go off continually for long courses of treatment. Despite all this it was not she alone who obstinately stuck out for the continuation of the marriage. Despite everything Wagner too was inseparably linked to her. She was the embodiment of his home, his comfort, his everyday life. He wanted to have both: the useful commodity of Minna and his exalted love for Mathilde Wesendonk. It was a strange travesty of the theme of *Tannhäuser*. In a later letter to Mathilde Wesendonk, written from Paris on April 10, 1860, he told her about the worries he was caused by the performances of that opera which had forced him to revise the Venusberg music, and he added to the recipient: "Don't be surprised that this happens in a letter to Elisabeth." Mathilde Wesendonk was thus Elisabeth to Wagner's Tannhäuser. The conflict existed just as much in real life as on the opera stage. And here too it could only end tragically, or at least in a way that was felt to be tragic. Nevertheless things finally turned out well. Mathilde Wesendonk later described the outcome: "The fact that until the master's death we were in friendly relations with him is subject to no doubt at all . . . We were never absent from the festivals at Bayreuth. After his marriage to Frau Cosima his first visit with her was to Mariafeld (where Herr and Frau Wille lived) and to the green hill at Enge, and on the latter visit he brought the children along."

The Wesendonks moved into their villa on August 22, 1857, but Richard Wagner had already been able to move into his house at the end of April. The idyll and the refuge on the green hill lasted almost exactly a year. Minna went away on several journeys, but between Wagner and Mathilde Wesendonk there arose a very close relationship that was a mixture of infatuation and intellectuality. Otto Wesendonk knew this and took care to practice the greatest discretion. Minna Wagner again suspected an amorous escapade like that with Jessie Laussot. Her attempt to ally herself with Otto Wesendonk against Tristan and Isolde failed, but the open conflict between the queens finally led to catastrophe. On April 7, 1858 a morning note to Mathilde Wesendonk was seized by Minna, who had bribed the gardener's boy. It was evidence of love, of jealousy, but also of strong artistic stylization. Wagner ended: "How I am babbling like an

Mathilde Wesendonk. Drawing by E. B. Kietz.

idiot! Is it the pleasure of talking alone or the joy of talking to you? Yes, to you! But as soon as I see your eyes I can talk no longer; then everything I could say becomes worthless. Everything is so indisputably true for me, I am so certain of myself, when these wonderful blessed eyes rest on me and I lose myself in them. Then there is no longer any object or any subject; everything is one and united, a profound, immeasurable harmony. Oh, there is peace, and in that peace the highest, fullest life! Idiot, who wanted to win the world and peace for himself from outside! Blind man, who had not known your eyes and had not found his soul in them! It is only inwardly, in the inward depths that salvation dwells. I can only speak and explain myself to you when I do not see you or when I am obliged *not* to see you.

"Be kind to me and forgive me my childish behavior yesterday: you were quite right to call it that.

"The weather seems mild. Today I will come into the garden; as soon as I see you I hope to find you undisturbed for a moment.

"Take my whole soul for your morning greeting!"

Once again a compromise was reached after all these scenes. Minna was sent off for medical treatment, and Wagner wrote extremely harshly and offensively to her on April 27, 1858: "This, dear Minna, is the date on which I have decided to have myself sent not to a medicinal spa but to a lunatic asylum—since that is where I seem to belong. With everything I say or write, even though my intentions are for the best, I arouse nothing but unhappiness and misunderstanding. If I keep silent about certain things, then I make you mistrustful and suspicious that I wanted to go behind your back; if I then write seriously and frankly in a way I thought—idiot that I was—would put your mind at rest, then I learn that I have been contriving a refined form of cruelty to bring you straight to your grave. At the same time I am told to be a man. Right, it is not just a man but your man that I want to be: only keep on telling me exactly how I should speak and think and see the things of the world, and I will want to keep on following these instructions and say, think and see nothing that isn't right in your eyes: are you happy with this? You can also always tell me what and how I should compose, write and conduct: I want to be guided by you in everything so that not for a moment longer can you have any doubts about me."

Social contact between the two families was broken off, but

the attempt was made at least to save the refuge. That too failed. A trifling episode brought the interlude to an end: Minna's return home from her treatment was celebrated by wreaths of welcome that now were to go on hanging over the door of the refuge so as to provide clear indication of what was and what was not legitimate here. Now it was Mathilde Wesendonk who lost patience, and Wagner had to leave. The composition of the music of the *Ring* had reached the second act of *Siegfried*. The composition of *Tristan* had similarly reached the second act. A draft of the libretto for *Parzival* (the spelling *Parsifal* only came much later) had been sketched out. Wagner left on August 18, 1858: first to Geneva, then to go on from there with Karl Ritter to Venice, where work on *Tristan* was to be resumed. This meant the breakdown not merely of permanent settlement in Zurich but also his marriage to Minna. An undated letter from Minna Wagner to Mathilde Wesendonk has survived.

Dear Madam,

It is with a bleeding heart that I must tell you before I go that you have succeeded in separating my husband from me after nearly twenty-two years of marriage. I hope this noble deed will contribute to your peace of mind and happiness.

I am sorry that by your very spiteful statements about me you force me to lay before you a verbatim transcript of that fatal letter my husband should have allowed himself to address to you: it was after reading it through that I finally decided to go to you to discuss the matter in friendship.

I hope you will now ask yourself what you would have done in my place. Firmly convinced that you had not misunderstood my noble good intentions the last time I saw you in connection with my talk with you I had however only too soon to learn that you were abusing my trust and had made it the subject of quite ordinary gossip. You repeatedly incited my husband against me and complained about me quite unjustly and inconsiderately to your own husband. When I returned after three months' absence my husband told me I must enter into personal contact with you. After a few outrages I agreed and was willing to cover what was past with the cloak of forgetfulness; only a loathsome rumor served to destroy this, leaving standing upright only the hope of retaining the Refuge, though this too was in vain, it was far too late—you did not want it and you were right to act in this way, it is the only thing I can thank you for.

Now Wagner will be working again, he who for so long was kept from this, which grieved me terribly.

As I had to learn recently; this is the only wish of an unhappy woman.

M. Wagner

Like Siegmund, Richard Wagner, who wanted to be a harbinger of joy, now had to find himself again cast in a sorrowful role. The Wesendonk episode between the rich businessman's wife and the poor artist in exile, set in a context of historical nostalgia for the Renaissance, could despite everything be tragicomic rather than tragic. But this does not apply to its artistic transmutation. *Tristan and Isolde* was a work at one and the same time classic and romantic, in no way indulging in nostalgia for the past but bold and new, tragedy and epic in one.

TRISTAN AND ISOLDE

Tristan is the first of the two major "interpolations." The libretto of the *Ring* had been completed, the score of *The Rhinegold* was finished, as was that of *The Valkyrie,* and Wagner had been able to set two acts of *Siegfried* to music before the great interruption started. But during the period in Zurich, the figure of *Tristan* had been emerging ever more clearly from behind the characters of the *Ring* cycle. The completion of *Tristan* and the *via dolorosa* that led to its first performance then drew in their wake, in a singular counterpoint of life and work, *The Mastersingers of Nuremberg.*

The genesis of *Tristan* is traditionally linked with Mathilde

The opening page of the manuscript of the libretto of *Tristan*.

Wesendonk. It is of course obvious that there are here immediate connections between life and its interpretation, between experience and artistic creation. Wagner said later of Mathilde Wesendonk in a letter to Eliza Wille: "She is and remains my first and only love." The artist's new emotions that up to then had only been guessed at but not genuinely felt (to the detriment of the score of *Tannhäuser*) were now transformed into a musical emotion without parallel.

All the same the identification between Mathilde and Isolde, Wagner and Tristan, Wesendonk and Mark cannot be successful. Certainly the artist who loved and renounced spoke later of Isolde and meant Mathilde Wesendonk; but occasionally he also called her Elisabeth. And it is hardly possible to blend Isolde and Elisabeth together into one person. Richard Wagner's love for Mathilde Wesendonk showed itself as a liberating force. It was indeed as a result of it that the world and the music of Tristan were able to emerge, but as far as Wagner was concerned it did not provide the first foundations for the world of Tristan: the essential elements of this latter had already begun to take shape within him. What the experience in the Norwegian fjord had meant for the *Dutchman,* the sight of the *Wartburg* for the genesis of *Tannhäuser,* the fracas at night in Nuremberg in 1835 for the future finale to the second act of *The Mastersingers:* this was what was provided for *Tristan* by Mathilde Wesendonk, a vision of life which released artistic motives already at hand.

The idea of *Tristan and Isolde* was in fact conceived not by a man in love but by someone conscious of his lack of love. As early as December 1854 Wagner had written to Franz Liszt: "Since in my life I have never enjoyed the real good fortune of love, I want to set up a monument to this most beautiful of all dreams, a monument in which from start to finish this love might for once be satiated: in my head I have planned a *Tristan and Isolde,* the simplest but most full-blooded musical conception; it is with the "black flag" that waves at the end that I want then to cover myself, in order to—die."

It was moreover important for the genesis of the new music drama that an internal relationship could be established be-

tween the themes of the *Ring* and the situation of *Tristan;*
Tristan was a consequence of Siegfried, and Tristan in turn was
to call forth the character of Parsifal. In a *Report in the form
of an Epilogue* which Wagner later published to give the history of the genesis of the *Ring* cycle, he wrote: "With the
draft of *Tristan and Isolde* it was as if I was not really remov-
ing myself from the circle of poetic and mythical insights that
had been awakened in me by my work on the Nibelungs. The
great interconnection between all genuine myths, as I began to
understand through my studies, had made me able to divine
clearly the wonderful variations which emerged in this interconnection once it was revealed. An example of this struck me

Tristan's death. Engraving after a painting by Piseis.

with delightful unmistakability in the relationship of Tristan to Isolde when connected with that of Siegfried to Brünnhilde . . . The complete similarity of this case consists in the fact that Tristan, like Siegfried, woos for another the woman destined for him according to the primeval law, compelled by an illusion that makes this deed of his an unfree one, and finds his destruction as a result of the tensions that arise from this."

However strange it may seem today, *Tristan* was to be undertaken with the intention of writing a success, a work that could easily be performed, with few characters and little demands in the way of scenery, and thus one that could quickly be staged in a large number of opera houses and redeem Wagner's desperate shortage of money. All the same he would soon have to say that, precisely because of the way the work was thus confined to the musical element and the internal drama, *Tristan* would be much more difficult to perform than all the elements of magic and sorcery in *The Rhinegold*. The antecedents of the first Munich performance of *Tristan* and the failure of the plan to perform the opera in Vienna after seventy-seven rehearsals demonstrated once again the contrast between the original idea for a work and the final definitive form it took.

The unusual effect of *Tristan* is not simply due to its having been interpolated into the genesis of the *Ring*. Nor is it remarkable only because of the almost grotesque discrepancy between the work as planned and the work as completed. Despite all the connections and interweaving of themes with Wagner's other works, it has remained unique to this day.

In nearly all of Wagner's works the isolation of a hero is immediately indicated by the title: *Rienzi, The Flying Dutchman, Tannhäuser, Lohengrin, The Valkyrie, Siegfried, Parsifal.* But the isolation is already broken in the title of *Tristan and Isolde:* it is the pair of lovers that stand at the center. The community between the lovers, which for both signifies a breaking out of their earlier isolation, is threatened not only from outside, by Mark, by Melot. It is also in danger from within, for love and guilt, the fulfilment of happiness and pangs of conscience are all too closely intertwined with one another. Even though this work presents a loving couple instead of the solitary hero in the title, it is continually threatened by new isolation.

More strongly than in his previous works, more strongly even than later in the *Ring,* this "love drama" circles round the occurrence of betrayal. Loyalty and betrayal are themes running through Wagner's life that he had to impress on nearly all his works. In *Rienzi* it still has a political meaning outwardly; in *Tannhäuser* it appears as a hesitation between conflicting principles; for the Dutchman and for Lohengrin it is a question of profoundest trust, of loyalty until death. The theme of betrayal in *Tristan* is in contrast more profound, more mysterious, and thus more fatal to all claims to happiness. This time Wagner has left the couple on the purely human plane. There is no contact between the world of men and the world of spirits. No longer does the tragic moment arise, as in the *Dutchman* or *Lohengrin,* from the breach of an other-worldly law that moreover cannot be kept. This time human relationships are threatened and betrayed.

Wagner's preoccupation in his Zurich years with the dramas of Calderón had had its effect. Wagner wrote to Liszt in January 1858: "Besides you and Calderón a look at the completed first act of *Tristan* I had brought with me has given me a wonderful boost these days." Calderón belonged directly to the subject matter of Tristan: love and betrayal are here fitted together as closely and indissolubly as love and honor. Wagner succeeded admirably in loosening Tristan's concept of honor from the noble milieu of the Spanish seventeenth century and using it as a dramatic motive without thereby devaluing the aristo-

104

cratic norms to a bourgeois model. Thus too the love potion only makes visible what was already in existence. It does not create the tragic conflict but merely helps to force it to appear. But the entanglement of honor and love allows no solution, other than forgetting.

The love-death of Tristan and Isolde is not to be understood as an obvious apotheosis, as formerly the union of the Dutchman with Senta. Tristan's mention of forgetting carries a different meaning. Much of Schopenhauer's denial of the world is contained in the sinking into unconsciousness that the union of the lovers brings about by the cessation of individuality. Here Wagner has taken up once again a romantic theme of E. T. A. Hoffmann and amalgamated it with the similarly romantic philosophy of Schopenhauer. Just as the love of the conductor Kreisler and Julia had renounced all earthly fulfillment, thereby following a postulate of love as it affects artists, so the twilight of Tristan and Isolde's love is only possible in the night-world of eternal forgetfulness. *Tristan* becomes the last and highest peak of German romanticism.

Its dramatic construction on the other hand strives after the most rounded classical form. Both the words and the music are a long way away from the love of romanticism for the fragmentary, for what is merely hinted at. There are three strictly constructed acts. First Isolde is at the center of the action; it is a long time before Tristan makes his appearance before her. The third act belongs to Tristan. The central act belongs to the loving couple: Tristan *and* Isolde. The two outside acts are marked by the day. Isolation and "bleak day" here carry the same meaning. The central act with its bringing of the lovers together belongs to the night, whose meaning unites forgetting, no longer existing, fulfillment and death. When the day breaks, new isolation begins for the lovers.

Dramatically the construction is based on the classical triangular situation of the French dramatic tradition, a tradition which is continued in the three-sided adulterous situations of French bedroom farce. To the triangle formed by Isolde, Mark and Tristan are added the confidants of French classical drama: Brangäne for Isolde, Kurwenal for Tristan. The role of Melot is that merely of the catalyst, but he too is linked closely with the major characters: to the king by loyalty and his betrayal; to Isolde by love, jealousy and betrayal; to Tristan by the loyalty of friendship and betrayal. And it is not only in its intellectual

content but also in its artistic construction that *Tristan* displays itself as a genuine work of the Romance tradition of the seventeenth century in France and Spain.

The music of *Tristan* also provides a unique blend of the classical and the romantic. It is at one and the same time bold and consistent. Wagner's contemporaries, and even the literary neo-romantics at the beginning of the present century, experienced the work as the highest peak of romantic emotional art. Modern musicology, by contrast, has rightly laid emphasis on Wagner's constructive skill and the classical exactness of the proportions of the work. The transformation of the feelings and actions of the characters in musical terms remains continually impressive. An example is Brangäne's song of warning in the second act which has to provide a contrast to the *Liebestod* duet. The lovers' song swells up in A flat major, rising in ever bolder steps, to reach its climax in the high unison A flat on the word "love." Brangäne's cry: "Take care! Already night gives way to day" is in G major. The contrast between A flat major and G major is linked with the slow but emphatic downward movement of the orchestra: the lovers, Tristan and Isolde, are as it were to be brought back to earth, to the realm of day. The simplest musical means are used to achieve a perfect correspondence of words and sounds, drama and music.

Another similar miracle is Tristan's death: the Tristan's glance motive, carried by the celli in the prelude, is once again sounded pianissimo and combined with the sustained notes of Tristan's last cry of "Isolde!" then to give way to the piano chord of the diminished seventh that indicates the breakdown of that glance. The helmsman's unaccompanied song at the beginning of the first act looks back to the helmsman in *The Dutchman* and the shepherd in *Tannhäuser;* but the folk song melody has become bolder and more astringent. The shepherd's ancient lay played by the cor anglais at the beginning of the third act is also without parallel in Wagner's work: this rhythm that mocks all symmetry and this enigmatic new melodic line has become a model for many great musicians of the twentieth century.

THE MINSTREL AND THE KING

WAGNER had left the little house on the green hill on August 17, 1858. The short period of security was over. More restless, wandering years now followed. Towards midday on May 4, 1864 he appeared for his first audience in Munich with King Ludwig II of Bavaria. The period between these two dates nevertheless abounded in plans and finished works: the music of *Tristan* was written in Venice and Lucerne, the libretto of *The Mastersingers* was built up layer by layer in Paris. Shortly before the final financial collapse, followed by the sudden and astonishing change in his fortunes thanks to royal favor, Wagner had these as yet unused artistic possessions to show: a score of *Tristan* which clearly went beyond all possibilities of performance in the demands it made; the two completed scores of *The Rhinegold* and *The Valkyrie;* two acts of *Siegfried;* and in addition the libretto and the most important elements of the music of *The Mastersingers of Nuremberg.* At first all this seemed to have been written for the desk drawer. At the same time the fame of his earlier compositions was growing. Wagner's success as a conductor had also taken on the form of a worldwide reputation. He was seen and heard in London and Paris, in St. Petersburg, Moscow, Prague, or Vienna.

Nevertheless these were years of restlessness, of irritation, of physical and mental decay. The former pupil of the Young German movement, of Proudhon, of Feuerbach, the man who as late as the beginning of the 1850's had firmly refused to link the Grail symbol in *Lohengrin* with Christian ideas, felt himself noticeably more strongly affected by religious ideas. They still lacked any unequivocal Christian sense: the Catholicism of Calderón was secretly compensated for by the heritage of Buddhism in Schopenhauer's thought. There thus arose an eclectic philosophy of life—changing the world and renouncing it, activism and transcendence.

The friends and acquaintances Richard Wagner moved among also had a different effect. In Zurich it was the well-to-do patricians, the artists, and the professors who formed the context of his social life. Now the former revolutionary and friend of Bakunin found himself increasingly in the company of monarchs and court circles of the most varied kinds. In Paris, in March 1861, there had been very tense intrigues between the imperial court of Napoleon III and the legitimist aristocracy as a result of a performance of *Tannhäuser*. Princess Pauline Metternich, wife of the Austrian Ambassador and daughter-in-law of the man who had chased the 1848 revolution out of his country, was Wagner's protector. Louis Bonaparte and the Empress Eugénie had wanted and demanded the performance of *Tannhäuser* which now, after a hundred and sixty-four rehearsals, in the presence of important friends of Wagner and with the newly discovered Wagnerian tenor Albert Niemann in the title role, was whistled off the stage by the aristocrats of the Jockey Club. Wagner, who had remained at home, withdrew the work. It was all the same a mixture of victory and defeat. A large section of public opinion, led by the imperial court, had declared itself for Wagner. It was not a crushing artistic failure but a theater quarrel of the kind that France had known for a century, such as the conflict of classicists and French romantics over Victor Hugo and his play *Hernani*.

The restlessness remained, but exile now came to an end.

German princes came together to make it possible for Wagner to return to Germany. The "Princess Regent of Prussia," Augusta von Sachsen-Weimar, intervened on behalf of the "converted revolutionary" in connection with a meeting between German princes and Napoleon III. King John of Saxony may have refused to allow Wagner to return to his country, but he abstained from vetoing when the culprit was allowed to stay in another country of the German federation. Wagner obtained a Prussian passport and was able to return. In Vienna he saw *Lohengrin* on the stage for the first time. He was greeted with wild applause and gave a brief speech of thanks from his box. Still, the years 1862 and 1863 were spent on the move. Wagner worked on *The Mastersingers* in Paris, felt himself drawn ever more strongly to Vienna, where the chances of a first performance of *Tristan* seemed to be most favorable. Early in 1862 he was amnestied by Saxony too. He traveled to Leipzig and to Dresden. Since his departure from Zurich he had in fact been separated from Minna, though there had always been visits and temporary periods together. At any rate the marriage had broken down. The last meeting took place in Dresden.

The Rhine near Mainz was able for a brief period to cast its spell over the wanderer. It was, however, not so much the world of *The Rhinegold* that captivated him as the link with the music publisher Schott, who wanted to publish *The Mastersingers* and *The Ring* and was willing to pay a lot of money for the privilege. And a new Mathilde appeared while work continued on *The Mastersingers,* who turned out to be the inspiration for the character of Eva just when musically it was needed. Mathilde Maier, then twenty-nine years old, came from Mainz. She was the daughter of a notary from Hesse, and her family lived at Alzey. Richard Wagner got to know her at the offices of Schott. Out of this grew a friendship that was reflected in a voluminous correspondence. Wagner addressed her merely as Evchen: Mathilde

110

Wesendonk had been both Isolde and Elisabeth for him. When later he settled in Munich, he wanted her to come and run his household: she turned this plan down, and in any case it had certainly already been thwarted by Cosima von Bülow.

Meanwhile in Vienna it seemed that for the first time it might be possible for the idea of performing *Tristan* to be realized. The tenor Ander was ready to take on the atrocious difficulties of the title-role. Wagner settled in the Austrian capital. Concert tours in Russia had been a tremendous success and had meant a net profit of 7,000 thalers. Now a new household was formed in Vienna, though without a housewife. Wagner had a housemaid and a servant couple.

The plans ended in artistic disappointment and financial collapse. *Tristan* was dropped as unperformable after innumerable rehearsals. Wagner could no longer rescue himself from his debts. Imprisonment for debt now threatened him. He sold the diamond ring of a Prussian princess, had to sacrifice the Érard grand piano too, finally had to make a rapid getaway and leave everything behind. On March 23, 1864 the fleeing bankrupt arrived in Munich, from where he traveled on to Frau Eliza Wille in Switzerland. There he stayed for the next few weeks. Once again he had found a refuge. On April 12, 1864 he wrote to Dr. Standhartner: "What am I to say? I am thoroughly miserable. I only know that a year from today I shall have the money to pay my debts; but for the moment everything depends on whether my affairs can be so ordered *for the present* that I get the courage and the desire to make something of my life. More I cannot say. *The Mastersingers*—just not to be thought of. Never! Never!"

But he could not stay any longer at Eliza Wille's either. Franz Wille, who had been in Turkey when Wagner arrived, returned: a Wesendonk situation seemed to be building up. In Vienna everything had been sold and put up for auction. Promissory

111

The time of sorrow was at an end. Richard Wagner was victorious. The miracle of Lohengrin had come about. But was it really a miracle?

It is with the entry on the scene of the young king, the knight "gleaming with brilliant armor," that Wagner concludes his account of *My Life*. He had reason for comfort. The final sentence of his autobiography was to remain true: "Under the protection of my exalted friend never should the burdens of the common pressures of life affect me again." Like Goethe's *Poetry and Truth*, this autobiography too closes with the minstrel being summoned by a prince.

In 1862, in the preface to the libretto of *The Ring*, the public was offered two possible ways of financing the complete composition of the cycle and its subsequent performance as a corrected whole. One way was "an association of art-loving men and women of means." But, thanks to what he had learned from his experience of patricians and bourgeois patrons, he did not seem to build very strong on this hope. The other way was as follows: "It would on the other hand be very easy for a German prince, who would not have to make any new charge on his budget for this end but would simply have to make use only of those means that hitherto had been allocated to maintain the worst public institute of art, his opera house that so deeply compromises and corrupts the musical intelligence of the Germans . . . Will such a prince be found?"

The call was heard. The young Crown Prince Ludwig of Bavaria, who had long been an admirer of Wagner's works and writings, had read the preface and taken it to heart. Now, since March 10, 1864, he was King of Bavaria. When on May 4 Richard Wagner, then only a few weeks away from completing his fifty-first year, entered King Ludwig's presence, he encountered a tall nineteen-year-old youth of unusual good looks. The correspondence that now began, if it is read in its entirety, has the emotional intensity of the music of *Tristan*. Ludwig

Ludwig II of Bavaria as Grand Master of the Order of St George, 1866.

began his letters: "Ardent beloved! Heavenly friend!" Wagner answered: "Dear one, loyal one, only one." Even at the height of the subsequent Wagner crisis in Munich the king signed himself: "In *eternal* love and loyalty till death, your Ludwig." Wagned signed: "Ever loyal and your own," or "Loyal and loving."

Eternal loyalty was invoked by the minstrel and by the king

only too often, even when the lofty style in which they wrote to each other had long since ceased to correspond to a profound friendship. From the start the alliance between artist and monarch rested on a misunderstanding. It was above all in the later decades up to the death of Wagner that Ludwig showed himself to be noble and kingly: he clung to the dreams of his youth and the royal summons he had once issued. Wagner meant more to him than merely a youthful longing: he was faithful to the one he had chosen, even though he had come to recognize that between the artistic creations he loved and their creator whom he was unable to love there existed a thoroughly unromantic division.

Wagner had royal gifts showered on him. All his debts could be paid off. The private budget of the king was at his service. A spacious house was taken at 21 Brienner Strasse. Earlier the king had granted his friend and favorite a country house on Lake Starnberg, not far from the royal castle of Berg. Wagner drew up a wide-ranging *Program for the King* that emerged as an artistic nine-year plan. For 1865 the premières of *Tristan* and of the still uncompleted *Mastersingers* were foreseen. The years 1867/68 Wagner reserved for a "grand performance of the complete *Ring of the Niebelung*." The program concluded: "1871–72 *Parzival*. 1873 My happy death."

Wagner's life and work in Munich were soon involved with conflicts on three fronts. The first difficulty lay in the all too great difference between protector and favorite. Ludwig was made to be a gushing admirer, not a masculine protector. Wagner had indeed ceased to be a democrat and socialist; he looked to princes for help in the realization of his plans; only he was himself a monarch, not a monarchist.

But as far as the king's Bavarian entourage and public opinion were concerned Wagner was still the revolutionary of 1849, the fighter on the barricades. This provided a second cause for tension. The cabinet secretary von Pfistermeister may have appeared in Stuttgart as the messenger of the king; nevertheless he was not in any way a Wagnerian but a Bavarian Catholic and an aristocrat loyal to the throne. For him, for the cabinet, and for the press Wagner was simply a dubious foreigner, a Protestant, a former refuge and revolutionary, a creator of incomprehensible and pretentious works of art, a squanderer of public funds.

In addition, Wagner's circle and also the king were pursuing their artistic projects at a time that in the historical field was concerned with quite a different set of principles. New forms of German unity were visible. The German war against Denmark provided a prelude; the decisive conflict for German hegemony was ever more clearly a matter involving the two great powers of Prussia and Austria. Bavaria was allied with Austria and therefore intensely anti-Prussian. Yet Richard Wagner had fetched Hans von Bülow from Berlin to be the king's pianist and court conductor; and Hans von Bülow—Berliner, Prussian aristocrat, and admirer of Heine—hardly let slip an opportunity to wound Bavarian susceptibilities. Moreover Bülow was an enthusiastic advocate of Bismarck: later at Triebschen, when they heard the news of the Prussian victory at Königgrätz (Sadowa) in the seven weeks' war of 1866, he together with Wagner and Cosima broke into cheers for Bismarck and cries of *"Austria est delenda."*

In this way, from the Munich point of view, the Wagner circle seemed to come between the king and his people, even between the king and his government. Furthermore, in keeping with his entire nature, there were no half measures about Wagner. Not only did he want the completion of his work, its definitive performance, and for this a special theater which Ludwig was to build on the Isar to the design of Gottfried Semper— another revolutionary!—who had been brought to Munich. In

117

"Only a passing visit": Wagner knocking on the door of the Bavarian Paymaster General. Title page from the Munich magazine *Punsch,* 1867.

addition he did not believe in leaving politics alone. His preoccupation was still art and the revolution, though it took new forms. His new writings that emerged between 1865 and 1867 were conceived as a "Mirror for Princes." Even in his first year in Munich the study *On the State and Religion* he wrote in 1864 was intended for Ludwig II and explicitly refers to him. The later essays *German Art and German Politics,* even though they appeared in the press in serial form, are unmistakably addressed to Ludwig II.

The audience had thus changed, and with it the relation of the writer to his milieu. Richard Wagner was well aware of this change in his intellectual attitudes, even though he also claims to have "really" said in all his earlier ideas the essence of his present views. This at any rate is how he is concerned to present the situation at the beginning of *On the State and Religion.* It is the same effort that exactly ten years earlier, when he discovered Schopenhauer in 1854, allowed him to present matters as if he had always been a Schopenhauerian without knowing it. Nevertheless there are irreconcilable contradictions between Wagner the former materialist and revolutionary democrat and the present essayist whose thoughts reach their summit in this thesis: "The designated quality of true religious feeling which, for the profound reasons that have been stated, is made manifest not through disputation but only through active example, becomes, when it is inherent in the king, the only revelation that is advantageous both to the state and to religion, and the revelation through which the two are related." Such accents are well-known from the time of Novalis, of the romantic counterrevolutionary theory of the state, of Frederick William IV of Prussia and the monarchist and state-church theories of Friedrich Julius Stahl.

The essays on *German Art and German Politics* look a great deal better. Here too there are many elements of "recantation." Nevertheless these essays contain a wealth of justified criticism of the hostility towards art shown by the bourgeoisie and the systematic adulteration and prostitution of the great values of German culture by a society based on profit. Once again Richard Wagner showed himself as the heir and guardian of the great German tradition of poetry and music, of Beethoven and Weber, of Schiller and Goethe. In impressive language he attacks the decline of artistic taste and the degradation of the greatest creations of German art to serve the end of providing cheap amusement. On individual details Wagner may be unfair in attacking Rossini's opera *William Tell* or Gounod's

Faust: nevertheless he emerges as a clearsighted critic of society when he shows that the German bourgeois public was only ready to accept Schiller's *Tell* and Goethe's *Faust* when they were rewritten in the form of tuneful operas. Although the critic of culture may emerge as farsighted when it is a question of pointing to symptoms of spiritual decadence, a chaotic lack of clarity reigns once again when Wagner presents the alleged causes of this decline and in his proposals for cultural renewal. But it is precisely because of its lack of clarity that this part of his ideas has become popular with the very German bourgeoisie whom Richard Wagner wished to bring to trial. The formulation that being German means "to do what one is doing for its own sake and for the delight in doing it" is repeated *ad nauseam* in these essays. A new and close association of education and religion is demanded. Then suddenly the supporter of Stirner and Bakunin again becomes noticeable: Wagner shows himself once again as an opponent of the state and wants to

Cosima, Blandine, and Daniel Liszt. Drawing by Preller.

120

play the king off against the state, which amounts to the identity of state and king and thus to the absolutist principles of Louis XIV.

So strong was the effect Wagner was able to have on Ludwig even from as far away as Triebschen that in the autumn of 1867 he managed to get him to finance a semi-official *South German Press* from the royal privy purse in place of the official *Bavarian Journal*. It was in the *South German Press* that the series of articles on *German Art and Politics* began. But on December 19, 1867 Ludwig himself forbade the further publication of the "suicidal" series.

There was thus conflict between the minstrel and the king caused by the difference in age and character. There were conflicts between Wagner and Bavaria. The third field of conflict was provided by the relations between Richard Wagner, Cosima von Bülow and Hans von Bülow. Wagner did not want to set up house in Munich without a lady of the house. Mathilde Maier did not answer the summons. Then Wagner had the Bülows brought from Berlin to Munich. First Cosima arrived with the children and moved in with Wagner on the Starnberg lake. Hans von Bülow followed later. In her diary Cosima later described November 28, 1863 as the day "on which we found each other and joined ourselves to each other." That was still in Berlin, where Wagner had visited the Bülows. On June 29, 1864 Cosima appeared in Wagner's country house on the Starnberg lake.

For Wagner long years of idle fantasies ended in peace. The daughter of Franz Liszt, the wife of Hans von Bülow, his pupil and friend, came over to his side. There was a much stronger entanglement of love, loyalty and betrayal than formerly on the green hill. Franz Liszt, his friend, was suddenly thrust into a new role; Hans von Bülow, who had come to Wagner as an enraptured disciple when a young man twenty years before, during the period of *Lohengrin,* was to take on the part of King Mark. Unpleasant lawsuits were conducted some decades later over which of Cosima's children were entitled to a share in the Wagner inheritance, and it appears that Bülow knew the truth by the beginning of the Munich period. Nevertheless he remained loyal to Wagner's work and to Wagner himself. His name is as closely linked with the first performance of *Tristan* in Munich, on June 10, 1865, as it is with the première of *The Mastersingers* three years later. Only Bülow's marriage was dissolved. Since Minna Wagner had died in January 1866, pressure built up towards a Bülow divorce and the legalization of relations between Cosima and Richard Wagner. In Munich, however, all this caused the king almost insoluble difficulties. There was society gossip; there were insinuations that King

Hans von Bülow.

Ludwig came to grips with in an open letter to Hans von Bülow with the aim of protecting Cosima's marriage; there was the king's profound disillusionment when he was forced to learn that he had been induced into proclaiming what was just not true. To talk of guilt or blame in this context is meaningless. Wagner's behavior was bound to offend against both the ecclesiastical and the bourgeois moral code; as far as his art was concerned he was still engaged in the middle of a battle; he was bound to be a scandal both to the legitimists and to his former revolutionary colleagues of 1848. But he himself—in his life, that is—had remained the disciple of the Young Germans, of Stirner, and of Bakunin. He had created the character of Siegfried, the breaker of all contracts, and seemed decided himself to infringe, for the sake of his work, all contracts and all links based on gratitude, friendship, or trust. When therefore he had to leave the Bavarian capital in December 1865 at the king's command, the king having been forced to take this step by the government and by public opinion, he felt secretly relieved. Financially he knew he was as secure as he had been before. Cosima was his. On Easter Monday in 1866, nine years after he had moved into his refuge on the green hill, Richard Wagner and Cosima von Bülow obtained possession of a villa at Triebschen near Lucerne, on a peninsula jutting into Lake Lucerne. It was here that *The Mastersingers of Nuremberg* was completed.

THE MASTERSINGERS OF NUREMBERG

FROM the very start *The Mastersingers of Nuremberg* was a great success. At its first performance, at the Munich Court Theater on June 21, 1868, Wagner was greeted by a storm of enthusiasm once the curtain had fallen on the final scene. And success stayed with *The Mastersingers*. The Berlin première on April 1, 1870 was, admittedly, a striking exception. The critics talked about "humbug" or spoke of "a dreadful yowling of cats, the result that would be achieved if all Berlin's organ-grinders were locked into Renz's circus with each one playing a different tune." But this did not put a stop to its success throughout the world. Nor did it in Berlin, where subsequent performances, which benefited from the lack of an organized group of anti-Wagnerians, had an increasingly friendly reception.

The Mastersingers has become Wagner's real festival opera. Nevertheless this element of musical festivity, which brings *The Mastersingers* close to Goethe and his view of opera as festival, was not enough. Another element was added: the possibility of the artistic expression of this kind of musical festivity had to become visible in Wagner's life and in his development as an artist.

The idea of *The Mastersingers* arose as early as 1845: the plot was sketched out and linked with the final speech of Hans Sachs, a first draft of which was also committed to paper at this time. If sixteen years later the idea of *The Mastersingers* could nevertheless come forward again, this happened at a time that offered the artist little opportunity to treat the subject of conflict between genius and audience in a more cheerful and inwardly self-assured manner. The score was admittedly completed at Triebschen as the work of an artist who was already victorious despite all the individual battles that were to arise. But the writing of the libretto and the invention of the nucleus of the music all belonged to a very difficult period of his life.

In a letter to Minna in the Burrell Collection dated February 14, 1862, Wagner wrote: "The time will come when, looking at a life like mine, people will realize with shame how

124

The minstrels' contest at the Wartburg. Detail from a mural by
Moritz von Schwind.

thanklessly I have been continually sacrificed to unrest and insecurity, and what a miracle it is that under such circumstances
I have created such works as for example the present one. But
as long as it lasts everyone thinks only of himself and regards
as most important the minor unpleasantnesses to which he is
subject." The work he was engaged on then was *The Mastersingers*. The rest of the letter's contents shows the final separation from Minna. She took it as a final letter of separation and

did not answer it. The marriage had finally dissolved. Money troubles were still with him; and Wagner was also without a home, even though he had meanwhile been amnestied and could return to Germany. But a remarkable counterpoint of life and work now made possible what then had remained fragmentary. Probably the failure of *Tannhäuser* in Paris was just as necessary to provide the impulse for *The Mastersingers* as the years of penury in Paris from 1839 to 1842, coupled with the experience of the Thuringian landscape, were in releasing the real impulse for *Tannhäuser* on his return to Germany.

In its completed form, too, *The Mastersingers* is to be understood as a counterpart to *Tannhäuser:* not of course in the form of a comic satyr play, but as a further development and companion piece to the earlier opera. Once again it is a question of opera and drama, foreign and German art, anti-Wagnerians and Wagnerians. The vision of Nuremberg was admittedly experienced by Wagner himself by the Pegnitz, seeing this well-preserved imperial free city with its unmistakable silhouette. But this experience of Nuremberg in real life provided only the visual setting for a spiritual antithesis that for its part, and not accidentally, was formulated and finally also cast into shape outside Germany.

In his autobiography *My Life,* in a passage where his resentment against the Wesendonks is still to be detected, Wagner describes how he had come to the decision to write this important new work in Venice, in November 1861, a few months after the *Tannhäuser* fiasco in Paris: "To cheer me up, the Wesendonks invited me to meet them in Venice, whither they had betaken themselves for a pleasure trip. God knows what was in my mind when I launched myself into the uncertainty of grey November and set out in reality first by train for Trieste, and from there to Venice by steamer, which also did not suit me at all, and occupied my tiny room in the Hotel Danieli. My friends, whom I found in very happy relations, were luxuriating in the enjoyment of the paintings and seemed to have disregarded the idea of chasing away my low spirits by enabling me to share in the same enjoyment. They did not seem to want to grasp anything of my situation in Vienna, in the way that generally at that time, after the unhappy result of the Paris undertaking that had been considered with such glorious hopes, I continually had to learn to recognize in most of my friends that they were quietly resigned to giving up further hopes for success on my part . . .

"I decided to put the writing of *The Mastersingers* into effect."

It was a remarkable conjuncture: the city on the lagoon where Richard Wagner was later to die was linked not merely with *Tristan* but also with *The Mastersingers*. In Wagner the experience of the southern world, the Catholic region, Italian art drew out of him its spiritual counterpart: German poetry, northern landscape, the spirit of an imperial free city, Lutheran hymns. It seems almost incredible, but it belongs completely to the work's genuine substance, when one learns from this passage that the crowd scenes of *The Mastersingers* had their origin in the surroundings of Paris, that the hymn with which the people greet the poet of the "Wittenberg Nightingale" in his own verses on the festival meadow came to the composer at the very spot of the Palais Royal where on July 14, 1789 the rebels had gathered to storm the Bastille. Nevertheless this apparent contrast between the surroundings Wagner was working in, the sources of his inspiration and the final form his work took is highly relevant.

The Mastersingers deals with Wagner's basic experience as a German musician in Paris. Wagner's art is equated with German art. Beckmesser on the other hand is aimed at Dr. Eduard

The Austrian music critic Eduard Hanslick.

Hanslick of Vienna, the friend and champion of Johannes Brahms and a passionate anti-Wagnerian. It was him just as much as Meyerbeer or the Paris opera merchants that Wagner had in mind in the resentment he expressed over *Jewry in Music.* Clearly recognizable in the delightful and basically harmonious art of *The Mastersingers* is the linking of patriotism with rabid nationalism, of German artistic self-assertion with xenophobic aggression. Nevertheless this is not a work of flagrant propaganda for a greater Germany. Hans Sachs's final speech is indeed the antithesis of this approach, with the distinction it draws between the power of the state and artistic greatness. With all its undertones, *The Mastersingers of Nuremberg* is a work of invigoration, not of confusion.

This too is connected with the process whereby it came into being, although not so much with the individual as with the historical development that was under way while Wagner was working on *The Mastersingers*. It was conceived in contrast to Paris, grand opera, Catholicism, and southernness. It was written in that decade of the 1860's in which, in the consciousness of the German bourgeoisie, the dream of German unity seemed to be coming closer to realization. The great Schiller celebrations of 1859 had already basically spelled the end of the Schopenhauer period in German intellectual life. Despair over the events of 1848 was beginning to fade. A new striving for unity was present among the people with Friedrich Schiller as its focus, often in the rather philistine form of Schiller associations and singing clubs.

German unity; but German unity imposed from above, through an alliance of princes under Prussian hegemony, confirmed in the three wars of 1864, 1866, and 1870/71. This element too is to be found in *The Mastersingers*. Already in this revolutionary speech on the relationship of republican efforts to the monarchy Wagner had talked of a revolution "from above." Everything was now repeated on a loftier stage and with a new historical topicality in *The Mastersingers:* the striving for German unity is reflected in words and music; but likewise unmistakable is the patriarchal and authoritarian factor. All that the people have to do in *The Mastersingers* is to provide ratification by a plebiscite; and to that it is summoned "from above." Basic laws of German history are brought to the surface here.

The sources of genuine scholarship for his comedy that Wagner held worthy of notice were only the references to Hans Sachs in Gervinus's history of literature and Wagenseil's chronicle "of the origin, practice, benefits and precepts of the gracious art of the mastersingers." Everything else was to be regarded as free poetic invention, and in this respect, not unjustifiably, he placed a very high value on his libretto. E. T. A. Hoffmann was also involved in the alliance: it is very easy to establish the influence of his tale of Master Martin the cooper and his journeymen.

Wagner distinguishes himself from the other available models for his libretto: the dramatic poems *Hans Sachs* and *Salvator Rosa* by Johann Ludwig Deinhardstein (1794–1859), professor of aesthetics and assistant director of the Vienna Burgtheater. Deinhardstein, for whose play about Hans Sachs Goethe had written a prologue in 1828 and whose text after revision for the operatic stage was set to music by Albert Lortzing in 1840, was a supporter of Metternich. His play too ends with Hans Sachs being crowned—but in the presence of the imperial majesty. The citizens happily rejoice "to a fanfare of trumpets and drums" and with the cry: "Hail Emperor Max! Hail Habsburg, hail for ever!" The similarity between the closing scenes is evident. It extends even as far as the stage directions. Deinhardstein's read: "In happy rejoicing the citizens throw hats, caps and banners in the air." Wagner's read: "While the apprentices clap their hands and dance in rejoicing, the people enthusiastically wave hats and kerchiefs." Only in Wagner the Emperor and the Habsburgs are lacking. Deinhardstein's emphasis on the duties of subjects in his play has been transformed into an apotheosis of bourgeois self-consciousness.

Every comparison of *The Mastersingers* with its sources must lead to the new and different element of civic pride becoming evident. But every modification affects the intellectual content of the comedy. With Hoffmann we remain in the bourgeois world of the townspeople: his tale ends with a marriage among townspeople. With Deinhardstein the world of the townspeople similarly remains on its own: warned in patriarchal style by the House of Habsburg not to presume above its station and to respect the bounds of the nobility. But with Wagner the knight Stolzing must prove himself as a mastersinger. Like the knight Rudenz in *Wilhelm Tell,* he joins the townspeople as one of them without privileges.

The aesthetic antithesis appears just as transformed as the political and social antitheses. Deinhardstein contrasted poetry and unpoetic pedantic formalism. In his original idea of 1845 Wagner was still quite close to this view of two kinds of art: a fertile art with its roots in the people, and one stiff with formalism. This was now fundamentally altered. Just as Wagner was becoming increasingly incapable of doing justice to contemporary music other than his own, so it must also have become intolerable to him to endure the opponent of his own view of art in the artistic sphere—even if it were in the form of "comic pedants." Added to this was the case of Hanslick, and his anxieties about a performance of *Tristan* in Vienna, linked with all the intrigues and faction-forming. Thus emerged the new Sixtus Beckmesser. The question is no longer one of fertile and sterile artistic creation: art and anti-art from now on stand in contrast to each other.

Wagner similarly goes beyond his sources in characterizing the positive principle of his drama. In his models Sachs and Salvator Rosa were the sole representatives of genuine art. To this Wagner brings the noble wooer from Hoffmann's tale and gains the contrast of Stolzing and Sachs, which is made to bear fruit in a double form with the contrast between Stolzing and Beckmesser and Sachs and Beckmesser. And this is not simply a question of dramatic construction. This time Richard Wagner's striving for identity is divided. Placed in contrast to each other, Stolzing and Sachs have the effect of an antithesis between the young and the mature Richard Wagner. The social synthesis follows the aesthetic one. Stolzing becomes a noble citizen. Moreover, he learns to combine the knightly art of Walther von der Vogelweide with strict observance of the mastersinger rules. As a statement of the facts of literary history this sounds absurd, but what is meant is not literary but musical history.

Hans Sachs possesses both qualities: youthful boldness and the experience of suffering. He is the true artist in the sense of this new Wagnerian aesthetic. But there is a twofold threat hanging over him. He is threatened by the possibility of drying up as an artist, and by the commandment of renunciation. This motive of renunciation also belongs to the side of *The Master-singers* that is influenced by Goethe. Besides Wagenseil and Gervinus, Hoffmann and Deinhardstein, Goethe's early poem on "Hans Sachs's poetic mission" must also be mentioned as a source.

In a unique combination, the German sixteenth century, reflected in the image of surviving Nuremberg, was contrasted with the nineteenth century that Wagner perceived as an epoch of decadence. *The Mastersingers* was to act as a warning. Beckmesser was the impotent, un-German world of opposition. He was "not the right one." Wagner's contemporaries must have experienced this climax of his operatic comedy as at the same

An anonymous late sixteenth-century drawing showing a candidate for the mastersingers (right) being examined by a board of markers (left).

time a national and social summons: an avowal of German unity and a call for a bourgeois democratic political system in which the knights became citizens. The political implications of this message must have been understood in Munich in the summer of 1868, two years after Bavaria's defeat in the war against Prussia, after the victory of the Junker Bismarck.

Friedrich Nietzsche's analysis of the prelude to *The Master-singers* has continually been quoted. It is to be found in *Beyond Good and Evil,* and opens the chapter "Peoples and Father-lands." The passage concludes: "This kind of music expresses best what I think of the Germans: they belong to the day before yesterday and the day after tomorrow—they do not yet have a today." But Nietzsche was wrong. The entire work of *The Mastersingers,* and the prelude quite especially, is inseparably linked with the present whose course imprinted the basic idea of *The Mastersingers* on Wagner the writer and composer. It is precisely because this work arose out of an unmistakable today, out of a final great experience of strength on the part of the German bourgeoisie, that it retains its power of illumination and remains alive. It is in a double sense that *The Mastersingers* offers a real world: it provides the real Nuremberg of the German sixteenth century; and in its entire artistic interplay it reflects the German reality of the national and democratic movement towards unity in the nineteenth century.

The construction of the prelude to *The Mastersingers,* and thereby the construction of the entire work, must be correctly understood. It begins with the motif of the townspeople's rights and privileges, embodied in the guild of the mastersingers of Nuremberg. Next the love and aspirations of the knight von Stolzing and the goldsmith Pogner's wealthy heiress runs their course alongside the mastersingers' world of art and citizenship. The character of Hans Sachs is conjured up: in him are embodied the townspeople's rights and privileges, understanding

The score of *The Mastersingers*. The opening bars of the prelude.

for youth, transfigured eros devoted to art. The characters on either side come to grips with each other: Beckmesser as the representative of the guilds' outdated ideas of life and art, and Stolzing's young knightly arrogance. The people decide the contest, put the marker to flight and press the young knight into the company of those men who have found their highest fulfillment in Hans Sachs: in a synthesis of loyalty to one's craft, active work, and professional standards in both craft and art. A brilliant flash of musical invention provided a unique musical expression for this attachment of the knight turned guildsman and master to an attitude to art and life embodied in Sachs in the contrapuntal combination of the three themes at the climax of the prelude to *The Mastersingers.*

At the same time, however, the music of *The Mastersingers* presents quite different and to some extent bewildering possibilities. The precedent provided by the score of Tannhäuser seems to want to repeat itself. There, the song style of the German artist Wolfram remained trivial, while the French world of Venus received a bold and brilliant expression. Here, the C major and the march style that appear whenever mastery and Germanness are to be described in the music no longer lend themselves to comparison with Wolfram's songs.

Only a secret affinity or ambivalence—as Theodor Adorno has noted, Beckmesser (and Mime) also represent Wagner's self-caricature—could have led to the fact that the same Beckmesser who is marked for artistic annihilation was represented by music that is now considered to be as fascinating as the musical world of the Venusberg. As early as the prelude, Beckmesser enters with a sudden modulation to E flat major, staccato, with eager and excited woodwinds, in the rhythmic diminution of the mastersingers' theme. His lute serenade in G major in the second act is admittedly in Wagner's reckoning meant to provide a contrast to the triad-based bliss of the prize song and, in the failure of verbal and musical accents to coincide, to present the opponents of Wagnerian musical aesthetics as absurd.

Yet Master Beckmesser's steps of a fourth refer to daring strokes that were seriously intended in the score of *Tristan*. The linking of the fracas theme, which is likewise characterized by steps of a fourth, with Beckmesser's own thematic material in the pantomime of the third act, is a musical invention of the highest order, and its effect today—quite contrary to Wagner's intention —is to provide a wholly positive contrast to the overdone repetition of the prize song.

In the score of *The Mastersingers* Wagner moreover discovered an enchanting synthesis of the earlier form of opera—that made up of separate "numbers" and the concept of the orchestra that provides a psychological commentary. The opera abounds with arias that—because of the dexterous text—have become speeches to other characters, monologues, prize songs. The tradition of the grand choral finale is retained, as is the traditional inclusion of a regular quintet. But the orchestra's psychological activity is also retained and further developed. Hans Sachs's painful sigh sounds in the orchestra in the first act at the words "Wait, masters! Don't be in such a hurry!" (played, in the same baritone register as the voice, by woodwind and strings but without flutes, oboes or first violins); it is then heard again in an expressive further development in Sachs's conversation with Eva in the second act, and finally in the cobbler's workroom serves to open the way to the master's inner world. Here one can judge the unity that was forged from inspiration and artistic skill in *The Mastersingers*.

RICHARD WAGNER IN BAYREUTH

WRITING to the King from Bayreuth towards the end of his life, on December 2, 1880, Richard Wagner admitted in retrospect: "Oh, the very fact of having discovered this good fortune; and yet to be able to say to oneself with a justified pride that in reality it must have been nothing less than a most gracious king and a wife like mine who preserved me not only for life but for the culmination of my existence."

It was the King of Bavaria he had to thank for his material independence, the luxury he enjoyed, his villas, the festival theater, and the most authentic performance possible of his music dramas. But only the victory over Hans von Bülow and the union of Richard and Cosima Wagner provided the foundation for the complete triumph. Cosima became guardian of the heritage Wagner left at his death. At this time the festival idea was still a project inseparably linked with Wagner himself: the festival theater seemed intended to serve as a setting for the first performances of his works. Once no more premières could be expected it seemed to have lost its function. The establishment of the Bayreuth festivals, the real completion of Wagner's thoughts, was the achievement of Cosima.

Cosima Wagner was not a misunderstood businessman's wife like Jennie Laussot. Nor was she, like Mathilde Wesendonk, a spoiled, late romantic patrician's wife. She was the daughter of Franz Liszt and the writer Countess Marie d'Agoult, and she belongs to the series of great women writers and intellectual catalysts who made a particular individual contribution to European intellectual life in the nineteenth century. Cosima Liszt,

Cosima Wagner.

who grew up in Paris with French as her mother tongue, had taken part since childhood in all the salon discussions on political and social demands and on problems of reform in the theater, in literature, and in music. She knew the separate worlds of her two parents, and later, after her sister Blandine married the politician Ollivier, she discovered the special world inhabited by the politicians of the Second Empire. She was born at Como on Christmas Day, 1837; at twenty she married the pianist and conductor Hans von Bülow, an aristocratic Protestant. In Bülow she found an interpretative, not a creative, personality. He was not able to stand up to comparison with her father, Franz Liszt. Then she came to know Richard Wagner, and here too a comparison seemed to force itself upon her that worked to Bülow's disadvantage.

Cosima was both sentimental and hard. Every performance of *Lohengrin* moved her to fresh tears of emotion. Her letters and actions were in contrast unrelenting. Her strongly marked aristocratic attitude contributed to this. Her own grandson, Franz W. Beidler, the son of Isolde von Bülow, noted that Cosima had been an opponent of feminine emancipation all along, with little interest in social theory, and with a decided sense of "order" and legality. "If it is true," he said, "that people of the nineteenth century can be divided according to their stand on the ideas of 1789 into the two major ideological categories of revolution and restoration, then Cosima Wagner belongs un-equivocally in the restoration camp."

The daughter of Liszt and the Countess d'Agoult had come to know socialist theories and theoreticians, doctrines of atheism and contact with the workers only when these were in a late stage of decline. The revolution of 1848 and the events leading up to it had no meaning for her: when her life began, the revo-lution in France had been brought to an end by the coup d'état of Louis Bonaparte, Napoleon III. In Germany the allied princes and kings ruled once more. It cannot be disputed that Richard Wagner's association with Cosima contributed essentially to the fact that the aristocratic outlook, élitism and an acceptance of inequality emerged ever more strongly in the artist's political views. From now on materialism and socialism were repressed; Schopenhauer, too, no longer basically fitted in so well with Cosima's campaign plans. At Triebschen and later at Wahnfried, the door opened to Count Gobineau and the ideas expounded in his *Essai sur l'inégalité des races humaines,* which reached their climax in an apotheosis of the Germanic race.

Thanks to Cosima and Triebschen, Wagner's creative work was from now on marked by stable continuity. It was on June 15, 1869 that Cosima first asked her husband to agree to a divorce and also to let her as the mother have his two daughters

Daniela and Blandine, and two days later he assented to this. Siegfried Wagner had been born a few days earlier, on June 6, 1869, so that there were now three children of the union between Richard Wagner and Cosima von Bülow: Isolde was born on April 10, 1865, at the time of the first orchestral rehearsals for *Tristan* in Munich; their second daughter Eva was born at Triebschen on February 7, 1867.

In Triebschen Wagner undertook the task of closing the gaps in his work and completing the fragments that had been left unfinished. In the summer of 1866, while war was raging between Prussia and Austria, between northern and southern Germany, a war that ended in a Bavarian defeat, Wagner completed sketching the music of the second act of *The Mastersingers*. The third act was ready in February of the following year, 1867, and on October 24 Wagner could announce the completion of the full score, which he sent the king as a Christmas present. The first half of 1868 was taken up with the première of *The Mastersingers,* and when that took place on June 21 Wagner was the triumphant hero in the royal box. Travels around Germany followed. On November 8, 1868, in the house of Professor Hermann Brockhaus in Leipzig, Friedrich Nietzsche was introduced to the admired Richard Wagner. On May 17 of the following year Professor Nietzsche, appointed to a chair at Basle, stayed at Triebschen for the first time. Meanwhile Wagner had completed the score of the second act of *Siegfried* and begun composing the third. In August the score of *Siegfried* was completed and Wagner turned his energies to *The Twilight of the Gods.* On July 19, 1870 the Franco-Prussian war broke out. In Triebschen Wagner was working on the score of the first act of *The Twilight of the Gods.* Meanwhile Cosima's marriage to Hans von Bülow had been dissolved. On August 25, 1870 Wagner and Cosima were married in the Protestant church in Lucerne.

Friedrich Nietzsche.

Under Bismarck's administration, the German Empire was proclaimed on January 18, 1871 in the Hall of Mirrors at Versailles. On March 15 Richard Wagner completed the score of his *Emperor March.* The second half of 1871 was devoted to the second act of *The Twilight of the Gods,* and the composition of the third followed in 1872.

During the stay at Triebschen all his plans were fulfilled. He had been able to complete both *The Mastersingers* and *The Ring of the Nibelung.* On April 24, 1872, Richard Wagner arrived in Bayreuth to settle there permanently. The foundation stone of the festival theater was laid on May 22, Richard Wagner's fifty-ninth birthday.

His old dream now took on shape. Already at Dresden, embittered by the activity of a repertory opera company, Wagner

141

had dreamed of a stage devoted exclusively to his art. Later he wanted to put up a temporary theater by the Rhine for a general popular festival of the arts, have the *Ring* staged there, and then immediately pull the building down again. Subsequently his plans and those of Gottfried Semper centered on a festival theater in Munich. Attracted by the beauty and individuality of the court opera house at Bayreuth, he traveled there with Cosima on April 16, 1871 from Nuremberg and a few weeks later informed the public of his intention of establishing the first Bayreuth festival in 1873 with a complete performance of *The Ring of the Nibelung*. The end of 1871 and the beginning of 1872 were taken up with his Bayreuth plans. From the start the city corporation supported the composer's schemes, but the first site chosen by Wagner for the festival theater turned out not to be for sale. The Bayreuth authorities decided on January 2, 1872 to build the festival theater on the present site. On February 1 Wagner acquired a site for a house for himself from the build-

Wahnfried, Bayreuth.

ing contractors Ludwig and Karl Stahlmann at a price of 12,000 guilders. There the villa Wahnfried was built, and Wagner was able to move in on April 30, 1874. His hopes had reached fruition. But at the same time his former fantasies had been buried.

This had already become recognizable with the Franco-Prussian war of 1870/71. The poem that Wagner wrote in January 1871, "To the German army before Paris," is not simply a bad poem as far as its form is concerned, but is at the same time an appeal to unrestrained conquest at the expense of France. Wagner now wrote a humorless skit deriding the Communards in beleaguered Paris, allegedly composed in the "ancient style" and thus after the model of Aristophanes. Is this merely a German patriot going temporarily off the rails in the excitement of the German Empire being founded and overstepping the bounds of good taste and humanity? It is certainly not only this. The Bayreuth program has the effect of an expansion of these polemical excesses. The *Speech for The Laying of the Foundation Stone of the Festival Theater* represented a complete break with Wagner's former plans for the realization of social progress. The national element is here closely related to the nationalistic; Wagner's view of human progress is now as follows: "The whole world today joins in the firm belief in what is termed progress, a process that is continuous and indeed in our day extremely effective, without ever really clearly considering where this progress is leading; on the other hand, those who have really contributed something new to the world have not been asked what their attitude is to a milieu of progress which has only offered them impediment and opposition. The unconcealed lamentation, nay the profound despair over this state of affairs voiced by our greatest spirits, whose creativity proclaimed the sole true progress, should not be recalled on this festival day."

It is the Bayreuth program of an autocrat, not of a former

democrat and socialist. Everything served to found a new religion of art: the writing of his autobiography, the publication of his collected works, the foundation of the *Bayreuther Blätter,* the patronage of the Richard Wagner associations. An unmistakable basic trait in all these activities is an antidemocratic, élitist praise of "inequality." Cosima encouraged this development. The first governess to join the household at Wahnfried reported that Cosima set great store in "presenting the children with the Habsburgs too in their history lessons . . . so that they may yet display greater interest for the Austrian Empire if we set foot on Austrian soil."

THE RING OF THE NIBELUNG

TWENTY-EIGHT years lay between Wagner's first adumbration of the Nibelung myth, written out in 1848 as *Sketch for a Drama,* and the first complete performance of the *Ring* cycle at the Bayreuth festival theater in the summer of 1876. It was not only the scale of the work as originally planned that had changed by being enormously extended, with the first dramatic outline entitled *Siegfried's Death* giving rise to a cycle of three music dramas preceded by a one-act prelude. The substance of the work had changed too, and the dramatized myth now had a function that was basically different. Nevertheless the kernel of the original idea was retained in the completed *Ring.* The different elements that were introduced over the years as a result of Wagner's development as a man and as an artist and thinker can without difficulty be distinguished from each other: it is only with an effort that the formal unity imposed by the leitmotiv technique can hold together the highly disparate parts of which it is composed.

Originally what was intended was to discover a way out of isolation. *Siegfried's Death* was not conceived as another drama about the artist and about the conflict between genius and society. In the first written draft the Nibelung myth is very strongly objectified: it bears witness far less to artistic self-assertion than to the foundations of a particular *Weltan-schauung.* The music drama, fed from mythological and folk sources, was to point the way out of the isolation that was at the heart of the dramas centered around the artist.

In the *Ring* the myth was to open the way to the people. Wagner had a thoroughly unhistorical understanding of "the people," seeing this concept as an absolute value, a substance that always remained the same. Hence he perceived all historical additions as unsuitable: only what was unhistorical and pre-historic was suitable. But since Wagner could not help under-standing the people as a social category (his reading of Proud-hon constrained him to this just as much as his acquaintance with Röckel and Bakunin), the myth had to retain a function in social theory.

In the world of Wagner's ideas of 1848 the Nibelungs were a "race sprung from the bosom of night and death. In incon-stant, restless activity they ransack . . . the bowels of the earth: they smelt, refine and forge the hard metals." A heavy burden on them, the workers, is the feudalism of the giants, who are unproductive. "But the giants do not understand how to use their power: it is enough for their gross minds to have bound the Nibelungs." The humanity of the gods is powerless here: "In lofty activity the gods now set the world in order, constrained the elements through wise laws, and devoted themselves to the most anxious fostering of the human race. Their strength stands above all. But peace, through which they achieved mastery, is not founded on reconciliation: it is accomplished by violence and deceit. The aim of their lofty world order is moral aware-

145

ness: but they themselves are gripped by the injustice they track down. Out of the depths of Nibelheim awareness of their guilt rumbles against them: for the Nibelungs' servitude is not shattered; only Alberich is robbed of mastery, and that not for a higher end, but the Nibelungs' soul, their freedom, lies uselessly buried under the belly of the idle serpent."

Hence Wotan's plan to allow a "free will, independent of the gods themselves," to hold sway and to break the spell. "In man the gods perceive the potential of such a free will." The remainder of the 1848 sketch corresponds in broad outline to the course of the action in the later cycle. The conclusion however had a very different appearance. Brünnhilde does admittedly give the ring back to the Rhinemaidens before she accomplishes her expiation by sacrificing herself, but no twilight of the gods follows. Her expiation liberates the Nibelungs and now, since the guilt has been erased, lays the foundation for Wotan's domination of humanity.

How close this is to the utopian socialists is unmistakable. Whether it is Saint-Simon, Fourier, or Proudhon is immaterial: their systems continually centered on the opposition of productive and unproductive classes in existing society. Wagner remained their pupil. It is the Nibelungs alone who are productive, though they are not capable of autonomy. What matters is for feudal despotism to be replaced by Wotan's humane rule. In Wagner's case a dictatorship of the Nibelungs is not to be thought of. Wagner's conception of the Nibelungs in its original version does not fit at all badly with his patriarchal revolutionary thoughts on the relationship between republicanism and monarchy.

The legacy of the Young German movement has its share in

A social evening at Wahnfried: on the left, Cosima Wagner with Siegfried; on the right in front of the window the conductor Hermann Levi; at the piano Franz Liszt. Lithograph by G. Papperitz.

the recurring themes of erotic emancipation, in the love of brother and sister between Siegmund and Sieglinde which alone can continue the race of the Volsungs. Siegfried and Brünnhilde too bear the unmistakable stamp of Young German heroes. Nor is the anarchistic element lacking. The "free will" in Siegfried, guiltless and violator of all moral laws, to which Wotan's humanity must appear as weakness, means nothing else than the victorious and liberating "egoism" of anarchist doctrine.

This basic myth now endured all the transformations that Richard Wagner had to undergo following his flight, living in exile between apparent security and fresh insecurity. Every new experience affected the basic concept a little. While Wagner was brooding over the boundaries between the categories of epic and drama, he became aware that too many epic narrations had to be introduced into the basic drama *Siegfried's Death* if one wanted to make the myth totally explicit. But completeness and explicitness contradicted each other: what would be gained in unity of thought would thereby damage the immediate understanding of the action of the music drama and therefore affect fundamentally its desired popular quality. In his famous letter to Franz Liszt in Weimar, written on November 20, 1851 at the spa Albisbrunn, Wagner sketched out his new idea which was to become the definitive final plan of the cycle: "I therefore had to communicate my entire myth, according to its profoundest and broadest meaning, with the highest degree of artistic distinctness in order to be completely understood; nothing of it anywhere should remain to be supplemented by thought or reflection: every unconstrained human emotion must be able to grasp the whole through its organs of artistic perception, because it is only thus that it can correctly assimilate what is most individual."

Moreover, connected with the new outline in Wagner's mind were thoughts of the particular problems of realizing it on the stage. At the same time as the plan of the four-part cycle there arose the basic idea of what was to become the Bayreuth festival: "The performance of my Nibelung dramas must take place at a great festival, which perhaps is to be established for the very purpose of such a performance. It must take place on three succeeding days, with the introductory prelude given the evening before."

The first alteration of the original basic idea was apparently still considered as an expansion of the former plan. In reality it was already to be understood as involving a modification. It affected Alberich and the curse of love. It was not by accident that in his letter to Liszt Wagner indicated the necessity of broadening the original scope of the drama in order to make this Alberich theme evident. In 1848 the love-curse might still be a mere element of the action: from now on in its new meaning it became spiritually significant for Wagner. The way to this new interpretation of the love-curse arose from his preoccupation with Antigone and the Oedipus myth. In *Opera and Drama* the reference to Antigone emerges from Wagner's consideration of the relationship between the individual and the state. Anarchist ideas continue to be highly effective. The Greek idea of fate is considered as "inner necessity from which the Greek, because he did not understand it, sought to liberate himself in the arbitrary political state." But this in the present was now "fate": Wagner indicates that the man of that time could only liberate himself from his fate by denial of the state. Antigone could serve as a model for this. Wagner concludes that it is only faced with the corpse of his son that Kreon, "the state personified," from being a tyrant becomes a human being again. The condition of being human, one has to infer with Wagner, could only arise out of the downfall of the entire political system of the state: "Blessed Antigone! It is you I now invoke. Let your banner wave that beneath it we may destroy and redeem."

Destruction and redemption—these already provide a transition to *The Twilight of the Gods*. *Opera and Drama* was written in the Zurich years in close intellectual proximity to the new idea of the Nibelung myth. Destruction of the state by free, unconstrained human love: this was how redemption was at first understood. This is still Bakunin and Feuerbach: in essence it means a development, but not yet a denial, of the ideas of 1848.

Then, under Schopenhauer's influence, the change is made from the active to the passive. Writing to his friend August Röckel in prison at Waldheim on January 25, 1854, Wagner strives to make evident the new interpretation of the *Ring:* "We must learn to die, and die in the fullest sense of the word; fear of the end is the source of all lack of love, and it is only bred where love itself is already fading . . . Wodan ascends to the tragic height of willing his downfall. This is everything we have to learn from the history of mankind: to will what is necessary and ourselves to bring it about."

Then follows a very striking passage: "After Brünnhilde's departure Wodan is in truth only a departed spirit: in keeping with his highest intention he can only leave things alone and let them happen as they happen, without ever again becoming decisively involved, and that is why he has now become the Wanderer. Look at him aright, and you will see he is like us to a T: he is the sum total of the intelligence of the present, whereas Siegfried is the man of the future desired and willed by us, who however cannot be made by us, and who must create himself through *our destruction*."

This is the first recantation: Wotan is no longer to rule, as in the 1848 draft, but is to open the way to the future for the new man. The second abdication is that it is no longer a question of shattering the state in order to redeem, but of seeking self-destruction in order to be redeemed. Siegfried however, as is indicated in this letter to Röckel, is the complete man of the future, because he has not learned fear and possesses the highest

Richard and Cosima Wagner, 1872.

degree of awareness—that is, to know that death is better than life lived in fear. Hence too he has no regard for the ring, and thus for power, because, as Wagner puts it, he "has something better to do."

But Siegfried thereby ceases to be a revolutionary or even an active liberator. Knowledge serves them all—Wotan, Siegfried, and Brünnhilde—only to know and will the end. Here the tragedy is transformed into a passion play. It is a preparation for *Parsifal*—via Schopenhauer. But at the same instant Siegfried loses the qualities of a tragic hero. His knowledge or ignorance and the actions that entangle him and make his murder possible are made to depend on the effect of draughts of remembrance or forgetfulness. This may carry the plot forward, but is a far cry from tragedy. And in *The Twilight of the Gods* Siegfried is given Christian, if not Christlike, traits. The way is open to late bourgeois drama. The popular myth of 1848 has taken on characteristics of a mystery play; and the spiritual and intellectual unity of the entire work has become increasingly questionable. In fact the *Ring* has three different conclusions—and thus no conclusion at all. There are three versions of the conclusion: one according to Bakunin, one according to Feuerbach, and one according to Schopenhauer.

The earlier interpretation of *Siegfried's Death* is eliminated. No longer is Wotan to rule, no longer are the Nibelungs to be liberated from slavery. The first conclusion of the completed cycle is Bakunistic: Walhalla is burnt down—and Wotan together with all the other gods. The rulers corrupted by the curse of gold and covenants meet their downfall so that the new purity of mankind liberated from gold can arise, even after Siegfried has had to be destroyed as a victim of gold.

Wagner, however, added to the published version of this scene some lines which were not set to music, and which now provide a second interpretation and a second conclusion. Brünnhilde declares in Feuerbachian style:

Like a puff of air
the race of gods has vanished;
without a ruler
I leave the world:
to the world I now allot
the treasure of my most sacred knowledge.
Not goods, not gold,
nor the splendor of gods;
not house, not hall,
nor the glamor of great lords;
not the deceiving bond
of gloomy treaties,
not the hard law
of moral hypocrisy;
blessed in joy and sorrow
let love alone be.

When Wagner published the libretto of *The Twilight of the Gods* he made known yet another, third set of lines from Brünn-hilde's final speech, and provided a kind of author's note to the reader in the form of stage directions: "Although with these lines the writer tried to provide an anticipated alternative for the musical effect of the drama, during the course of the long interruptions that kept him from completing the composition of his text he felt him-self moved to a version of this final poem of departure that corre-sponds still better to that effect, and this too he now appends." This new interpretation is to be found in the following lines:

Now that I go no longer
to the fastness of Walhalla
do you know where I am going?
I am leaving the home of wishes,
the home of delusion I am fleeing forever;
behind me I close
the open gates
of eternal becoming;
to the chosen land
beyond wish and delusion,
goal of world-wandering,
now goes the knower.

Do you know how I won
the blessed end
of everything eternal?
The deepest suffering
of sorrowing love
opened my eyes:
I saw the world come to an end.

This, however, is unmistakably Schopenhauer. It no longer has anything to do with the protest of 1848, or with Wagner's interpretation of the burning of Walhalla, or with the basic anti-capitalistic idea.

The transitional character of this enormous work can be observed from numerous details. Alberich's love-curse points both to the third act of *Tristan* and to Amfortas' curse of love in *Parsifal.* The erotic links between the Volsungs Siegmund and Sieglinde or also between Siegfried and Brünnhilde are closely related to the Young German emancipation of love. It is only from anarchy that there is everywhere a retreat—with the help of Schopenhauer and going beyond him—so that it becomes something that is not binding on society even if desired. The continuity and discontinuity in Wagner's thought are in no other work in such close proximity as in *The Ring of the Nibelung.*

Music of the highest inspiration and of extraordinary artistic skill can wash over contradictions in the momentary context of experiencing the work in the theater. Essential for Wagner was the epic element supplied by the orchestra in the musical drama, the psychological interpretation of what was happening on the stage by means of the orchestral accompaniment and the purely orchestral passages, the linking of the action on the stage with its roots and reflections in the past which the orchestra contributes from time to time. But interest in a performance of the *Ring* in our day is without a doubt reserved for the great lyric episodes, the descriptions of nature or of emotions without any element of psychological explanation. Water and fire, storm and tempest, work rhythms and forest murmurs, love song and funeral march: these have become the central points of the audience's experience, because at the same time they represent the musical climaxes. Themes that press forwards, visible as an upward movement in the score, are understood as courage, heroism, lack of anxiety. Depression and pessimism, as in the motives of anxiety, brooding, and also the twilight of the gods, appear as a downward movement.

The popular character that is aimed at in this mythological art never in fact finds expression in the scenes involving the people, that is in the vigorous choral sections. The genuine popular character of a Handel oratorio with its powerful choral passages stands in the sharpest contrast to the forced popular character in Wagner's work, which brings into the action only gods, demons, or heroes and antiheroes but confines "vassals" to episodes where the choir sings its agreement, as previously in *Rienzi* and *Lohengrin* and for the first time fully in *Tristan*. And again as in *Tristan* this music's final message is one of downfall, not of victory. The work lives in the painful beauty of remembering, of looking back.

Hence two musical climaxes of the entire cycle stand in a close relationship to each other: the opening of the whole work in *The Rhinegold* and the funeral march in *The Twilight of the Gods*. In the former there is the highest degree of simplicity and purity in the musical expression and meaning; in the latter the fullest complexity of interrelationships as a retrospective summing up of a human life and its conditioning factors, presented as music of the uttermost interlacing and interweaving of motives. This indeed was what Wagner had sought. In this music, which begins with C minor chords and the chromatic rise and fall of the death motive, then to unite together all the

155

motives of Siegfried's life from the love song of his parents to the shattering of his heroism, is to be found only what is past and what is remembered. The scene is set at night, the moon breaks through the clouds, the happiness and joy of youth are remembered, then the mists rise up from the Rhine and cover the scene. The drama is at an end: the orchestra provides the final epic statement. It is here, and only here, that the musical tragedy finds its expression: in music without any accompanying action on the stage. The rest is the music dying away and theatrical effect, though with the "festival of relationships" repeated once again, but not surpassed, in Brünnhilde's final speech. The music too failed to force the three conclusions of the *Ring* cycle together to form a unity.

PARSIFAL: TRANSFIGURATION AND DEATH

AT the end came the great recantation. The laying of the foundation stone of the Bayreuth festival theater was celebrated with a performance under Wagner's direction of Beethoven's Ninth Symphony in the court opera house. But in this last decade of his life Wagner's own activity was revealed more and more, to quote Adrian Leverkühn's phrase from Thomas Mann's *Doctor Faustus,* as a "recantation" of this very Ninth Symphony. The foundation of what may be termed a Church of Bayreuth and of Wagnerian theology, the requirement of being addressed as "master," the final culmination of *Parsifal*—everything seemed to negate the way that had been taken by art and philosophy in the preceding century: the way of secularization. The plea for peace in the *Missa Solemnis* referred to peace on earth; the Ninth Symphony, that synthesis of Schiller and Beethoven,

156

The Bayreuth Festival theater.

understood the appeal to the creator, to God, largely in symbolic terms; Ludwig Feuerbach had declared (and Wagner had followed him in this) that the heavenly family was nothing other than a projection into the hereafter of images of earthly families. All this was now recanted by Wagner.

August 1876 brought the first Bayreuth festival and the massed arrival of princely guests. Wagner gathered around him the loyal followers from the different periods of his life: the Wesendonks; Mathilde Maier; Liszt too appeared, and was concerned to restore, at least with regard to external appearances, his long ruffled relations with his daughter and son-in-law. King Ludwig arrived at night with his entourage and for the first time for eight years found himself once more alone with Richard Wagner. He attended the festival but then left immediately so as not to have to meet his new overlord, Wilhelm I, the victor of 1866. Richard Wagner received the king of Bavaria, the emperor of Germany, the emperor of Brazil, the king of Württemberg, princes, notables, artists from all over the world. It had turned out anything but the popular festival that had once been dreamed of in Zurich. To be sure, the work that was performed here, the *Ring* cycle, was not exactly created to be the art of the greatest popular appeal.

Friedrich Nietzsche recognized this increasingly clearly. His friendship with Richard and Cosima Wagner had in fact not continued past Triebschen. Clashes already began to arise at Bayreuth. The philosopher placed Brahms's *Song of Triumph* on the piano in Wahnfried. Wagner threw it aside in a rage: "Handel, Mendelssohn and Schumann bound in leather!" Brahms as a rival god was not to be tolerated, all the less so since Hans von Bülow, the conductor and admirer of Wagner, had gone over to Brahms. Brahms meant the contrary art to Wagner's own, in other words: Mendelssohn, Schumann, and Handel. All this was already part of the Church of Wagner.

Nevertheless Wagner did not think of demonstrating a stylized Olympia attitude. The relationship between him and the Frenchwoman Judith Gautier formed a private counterpoint to the festival month of August 1876. She was the daughter of Théophile Gautier and the wife of the writer Catulle Mendès, and knew Wagner from his Triebschen days. She was still young, on friendly terms with Cosima, very intelligent and musical, and a passionate propagandist for Wagner's art in France. It was not a great love affair. It was a matter of play, frivolity, pleasure; occasionally the correspondence shows attentive, almost caressing old man's letters. All this took place behind Cosima's back. Once again an entanglement was woven of love, friendship and betrayal, but the strong accents of *Tristan* were lacking.

The festival ended with an immense deficit. Repeat performances were hardly to be expected for the following years; long drawn-out financial negotiations were needed to pacify the subscribers and patrons. Since the northern climate suited his health less and less, Wagner now preferred to live in Italy. In November 1876, at the villa of Malwida von Meysenburg in Sorrento, a final meeting took place between Wagner and Nietzsche.

Elisabeth Förster-Nietzsche, whose testimony should be handled with caution, especially because her feelings of resentment against Cosima are only too strongly noticeable, claims to have preserved a remark of Wagner's dating from that time: "The Germans now do not want to hear anything of heathen gods and heroes, they want to see something Christian." This refers to the deficit incurred by the festival, but also to the prevailing mood and spirit of 1876. The five billion gold francs of French war reparations had unleashed in the economy of the German empire a vast speculative boom, which was now followed by the ensuing crisis. Twenty years earlier Schopenhauer's pessimism had fitted the mood of the time: now there seemed to announce itself a Christianity fitted to the times which Nietzsche thought to oppose but which Wagner, in this new phase of his life and creative work, came a long way to meet.

The writing of *Parsifal* too had its origins in a vision dating back to Good Friday of the year 1857. Wagner stood in front of his house and looked at the spring landscape by the lake of Zurich: Good Friday morning and nature in bloom. This was the cell from which the festival opera was later to grow: at the same time a musical climax was provided for the score of

159

Parsifal. Wagner wrote out the course of the action as an epic tale in the last days of August 1865. As far as Wagner was concerned it was natural to turn to this final labor once the Bayreuth performances were over. Writing from Bad Ems on July 22, 1877 he told the king of the completion of the libretto. Then the composition of the music began. In the afternoon of May 3, 1879 the king received a telegram that had been handed in at Bayreuth shortly beforehand:

> Third of May! Gracious May!
> 'Tis you with praise I greet:
> Winter's sway has passed away,
> and Parsifal's complete.

Does *Parsifal* signify a break in the tradition of Wagner's life? The first impression is one of overwhelming spiritual and intellectual continuity. There is hardly a theme running through Wagner's life and work that does not recur here. Like Tannhäuser, Parsifal stands between heavenly and earthly love; like Lohengrin, he strives to struggle free from earthly feelings. Like Siegfried, Parsifal is the pure fool: the opponent of arguments, questions, statements. Pure subjectivity and pure action provide the German mixture that Wagner holds suitable for Siegfried as for Parsifal. Amfortas points backwards to Tannhäuser and Tristan. Kundry is a combination of Venus and Elisabeth, Young German nymph and saint. Klingsor's love-curse points to Alberich. Gurnemanz's knowledge is of the same class as Wotan's, similarly without hope and impotent.

The mystery-play character of *Parsifal* has also already been foreshadowed in the *Ring.* The world of men is taken only in a symbolic, no longer in a real, sense; and thereby all possibility of genuine tragedy is lost. Wagner's early works from *The Dutchman* onwards offered the romantic contrast between the world of men and the world of spirits. *Tristan* and *The Master-*

Richard Wagner, 1882.

singers were however fixed only in the here and now, among
human beings. In *The Ring of the Nibelung* tragedy existed
wherever men suffered at each other's hands without gods and
destiny being able to guide events: once the gods exercised their
miraculous powers the context of tragedy was dissolved. Tragedy
was provided by Siegmund's love for Sieglinde, but not by Siegmund's death. In *Parsifal* Wagner is alarmingly consistent: it
is only what is divine that is decisive, in all his actions and erring
man serves only the preordained plan of salvation. But this

means losing all possibility of being moved by human action and suffering; veneration is to be paid only to the transcendent. This means appealing to an extra-artistic tribunal.

While he was composing the music of *Parsifal* Wagner wrote to Judith Gautier: "Help me . . . hold me dear; but for that we do not want to wait for the Protestant heaven, since it certainly will be very wearisome there." Yet a remarkable combination of ideas—*Parsifal* represents the private theology of Richard Wagner, a mixture distilled from ancient Persian, Indian, and Christian mysteries, from Young German sensuality and Schopenhauer's philosophy of the redemption of the world —had the effect that the festival opera which showed such strongly Catholic-inclined traits remained simultaneously bound to a harsh Calvinist doctrine of predestination. Everything is decided in advance in accordance with a fixed plan of salvation: the redemption of Kundry and of Amfortas, Parsifal's decision between sensual pleasure and peace of soul. As soon as the unknown though foreordained redeemer is mentioned he appears. Theatrical dexterity is linked with a theology that strongly denies free will. Much more intensely than in the *Ring* the tragic interplay of action, and bourgeois tragedy too, has been transformed into the passion play.

For this reason too Kundry or Amfortas cannot be seen as genuinely tragic figures. Kurt Hildebrandt, the follower of Nietzsche, who learned from his master how to cast the evil eye on to Wagner's weaknesses, saw Kundry as "the hysterical sleepwalker, the mis-shapen character grunting like an animal-woman as the archetype of sin." His view of her erotic aspect is: "Baseness invented from abstract sophistry, without animal vigor, is intolerable." There is something in this. Kundry is a remarkable dramatic character: Thomas Mann found her extremely interesting, which should not be surprising. Nevertheless she is far more an idea than a character. Her male counter-

Wagner's study at Wahnfried.

part in Wagner's work, the flying Dutchman, was a ghost with human traits: the causes of the curse receded before the suffering brought about by his wandering.

Amfortas is a Lohengrin after true union with Elsa. His humanity has been victorious over his spiritual office. This could provide a tragic conflict: that, as it were, of the sinful priest.

But the controlling plan of salvation prevents this having any really shattering effect. Amfortas must sin so that he can be absolved: all decisions are understood only as foreshadowings of the conditions for Parsifal's appearance, and the course of that too is similarly fore-ordained...

The music is however more than this. Admittedly it makes much use of tried and tested procedures. The prelude attempts as it were to combine the effects of the prelude to *Lohengrin* and the opening of *The Rhinegold:* this time the atmosphere of the grail is not summed up by the brilliance of violins hovering downwards in A major, but instead long sustained notes in A flat major deep in the lower strings rise upwards like the primeval experience of the start of *The Rhinegold.* The orchestration is masterly throughout and for long stretches serves to conceal a certain scantiness of proper musical inspiration. Nevertheless it would be wrong to label the continual recurrence of the same motifs as indicating a poverty of inspiration in the aged Wagner, as has often been done. Repetition is here a liturgical, static factor, an element of conservation. Repetition means teaching those not yet of age—until even the most obtuse listener has grasped what the leitmotivs are for.

Side by side with the effect of simplicity that is sought in the music there are examples of extreme harmonic boldness. Parsifal's reel away from Kundry's embrace, with a downward chromatic movement of quavers accompanied by an upward movement of dotted quavers in similarly chromatic steps, the cry "Amfortas! The wound!", the confused rising and falling of the orchestral figuration: all this is quite unusual and unique. But the conventional transfiguration of the conclusion, with A flat major and D flat major and A flat major and the grail glowing red and the mystical chorus, remains hard to bear. All the complaints that since the first performance have been leveled against this kind of theatrical substitute for a church

164

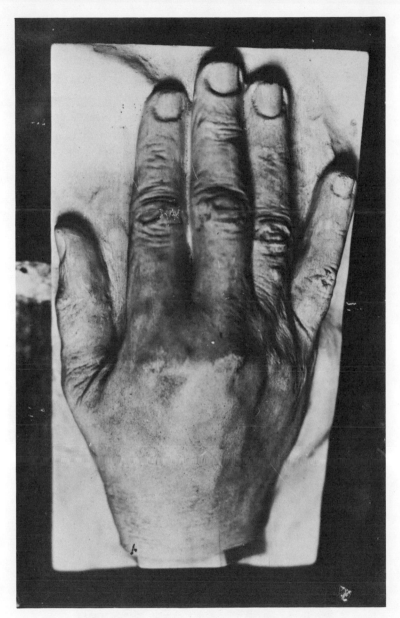

Plaster cast of Richard Wagner's right hand.

service have been confirmed, not refuted, by subsequent generations.

The first performance of *Parsifal* took place in the festival theater on July 26, 1882. King Ludwig did not attend. Wagner had beseeched him to come in a letter of July 8, had even suggested a special performance, but despite all his submissive phraseology had decisively rejected the demand to have *Parsifal* performed for the king in Munich. In November 1880 he had conducted the prelude to *Parsifal* for Ludwig in Munich, but then let the Munich conductor Hermann Levi conduct the encore demanded by the king. And it was Levi whom he brought to Bayreuth to conduct the first performance of *Parsifal,* despite

The conductor Hermann Levi, under whose baton *Parsifal* was given its first performance.

his ideas about "Jewry in Music." In November 1880 Ludwig and Wagner, the minstrel and the king, saw each other for the last time. A year later the *Ring* cycle was performed for the first time outside Bayreuth, in Berlin. Wagner and Cosima were present. Shortly afterwards Cosima met Hans von Bülow to discuss the fate of their two eldest daughters. Sixteen performances were given: the social setting corresponded to that of the first Bayreuth festival in 1876. At the last performance Wagner, unseen by the audience, appeared in the depths of the orchestra pit to conduct the final act himself. Afterwards he was very sad and filled with forebodings of death.

His final report and his speech to the artists did however end with hopes of another performance in 1883. Then Wagner undertook his final journey to Italy.

Eighteen rooms on the top floor of the Palazzo Vendramin

The Palazzo Vendramin, Venice.

in Venice were rented. Here his last writings were committed to paper. For a long time Wagner had refused to confine his writings to questions of art, of his art. The claim to universal validity, to acceptance of his ideas without contradiction, had in fact led him since his arrival in Bayreuth to dominate the scene there to proclaim his views on all questions. This inevitably gave rise to unconscious humor. Thus his 1880 essay on *Religion and Art* contains the following astonishing decree: "Nevertheless one could even regard contemporary socialism as very much worthy of consideration by our political society, and this indeed for strong inner reasons, provided it is truly and inwardly united with the three associations considered beforehand, of the vegetarians, for the protection of animals, and of the temperance movement."

An open letter to Heinrich von Stein, signed at Venice on January 31, 1883, shows Wagner as all too loyal a pupil of Gobineau's racial doctrine. The German races are "granted, by going back to their roots, a competence which has been lost by the entire Semiticized so-called Latin world." This is the final form taken by the conflict arising from his years of starvation in Paris from 1839 to 1842. He had also retained his ideas of anarchy. The sketch for a future of society that Wagner drew up a fortnight before his death is able to adduce "church and state . . . only as examples of a terrible warning." Anarchy is linked with his own Wagnerian theology. Bayreuth could not tolerate any other Church near itself.

On January 13, a month before Wagner's death, Liszt left the Wagner family with whom he had been spending the winter till then in order to travel to Budapest. In the afternoon of February 13 Richard Wagner succumbed to a heart attack. On his desk lay an uncompleted manuscript *On the Feminine Aspect of Humanity:* it was conceived as a final contribution to his essays on religion and art. The last sentences that Wagner wrote

Letzte Bitte
an meine lieben Genossen.

! Deutlichkeit!

Die grossen Noten kommen von selbst; die kleinen Noten und ihr Text sind die Hauptsache. —

Nicht dem Publikum etwas sagen, sondern immer dem Andern; im Selbstgespräche nach unten oder nach oben blickend, nie gerad' aus. —

Letzter Wunsch:
Bleibt mir gut, Ihr Lieben!

Bayreuth, 13 August 1876.

Richard Wagner

Wagner's "last request," written on August 13, 1876, seven years before his death.

led back to his beginnings, to the world of young German sensuality and feminine emancipation, to his early opera *The Ban on Love:* "Nevertheless the process of the emancipation of woman takes place only with ecstatic convulsions. Love—tragedy."

Wagner's body was brought from Italy to Germany solemnly escorted with royal honors. At the Bavarian frontier the funeral procession was received by King Ludwig's representative and the king's wreath added to the tributes. In Munich too an enormous crowd was waiting. The king did not appear. The cortège was received in Bayreuth and conducted to Wahnfried, where the children awaited the coffin. Cosima did not take part in the burial. Franz Liszt, too, did not turn up. The entire city honored its citizen Richard Wagner, but nevertheless the director of the theater, Angelo Neumann, wrote: "To me it was as if a god had departed from us; and everything that took place in Bayreuth could just as well have served for some valiant citizen of this town."

CHRONOLOGY

1813	May 22: Richard Wagner born in Leipzig, son of the police official Carl Friedrich Wilhelm Wagner. November 23: Father dies.
1814	August 28: Wagner's mother marries the actor and writer Ludwig Geyer. The family moves to Dresden.
1822–27	Wagner attends the Kreuz school in Dresden.
1828–30	St. Nicolaus school in Leipzig.
1830	St. Thomas school in Leipzig.
1831	Matriculates at Leipzig University as a music student. Pupil of Theodor Weinlig.
1833	Chorus master at Würzburg.
1834	Summer: Director of music of the theatrical company at Lauchstädt.
1834–36	Director of music at the theater at Magdeburg.
1836	November 24: Wagner marries Minna Planer at Tragheim near Königsberg.
1837	April 1: Becomes director of music at the theater in Königsberg. August 1: Arrives in Riga and occupies post as director of music at the theater there until 1839.
1839	The Wagners arrive in Paris after a stay in London.
1840–42	Wagner in Paris. Writings published in *Gazette musicale de Paris*.
1842	Wagner returns to Germany. October 20: First performance of *Rienzi* at the Dresden Court Theater.
1843	January 2: First performance of *The Flying Dutchman* at the Dresden Court Theater. Appointed conductor to the Royal Saxon Court.
1844	Conducts the first Berlin performance of *The Flying Dutchman*.

171

1845	October 19: First performance of *Tannhäuser* at Dresden.
1846	April 5: Conducts Beethoven's Ninth Symphony for the first time in the Old Opera House, Dresden.
1849	May: Takes part in the revolution at Dresden. A warrant is issued for Wagner's arrest and he goes into exile in Zurich.
1850	Travels in France. Affair with Jessie Laussot. August 28: First performance of *Lohengrin* at Weimar Court Theater.
1852	Becomes acquainted with Otto and Mathilde Wesendonk. (Summer) Journey through upper Italy.
1853	May: Concerts of Wagner's works in Zurich. July 2: Franz Liszt arrives in Zurich.
1855	Conducts eight concerts in London.
1857	Moves into the "refuge on the green hill" near Zurich supplied by the Wesendonks. Entertains Hans and Cosima von Bülow while they are on their honeymoon in Zurich.
1858	Leaves Zurich and goes to Italy.
1859	Returns to Switzerland and travels to Paris.
1860	Three concerts in the Italian Theater in Paris. Concerts in Brussels. Partial amnesty by the King of Saxony; returns for the first time to Germany.
1861	March 13: First Paris performance of *Tannhäuser*.
1862	Leaves Paris and returns to Germany. Stays in Mainz, Biebrich, Karlsruhe, Dresden, and Vienna.
1863	Concerts in St. Petersburg, Moscow, Budapest, Prague, and Karlsruhe.
1864	May 4: First meeting between King Ludwig II and Wagner. Wagner moves to Munich.
1865	June 10: First performance of *Tristan and Isolde* at the Munich Court Theater, conducted by Hans von Bülow.
1866	January 25: Minna Wagner dies at Dresden. Moves into villa at Triebschen near Lucerne.
1868	June 21: First performance of *The Mastersingers* at the Munich Court Theater. November 8: Wagner meets Friedrich Nietzsche in Leipzig.

172

1869	June 6: Siegfried Wagner, the third child of Richard Wagner and Cosima von Bülow, is born. September 22: First performance of *The Rhinegold* in Munich.
1870	June 26: First performance of *The Valkyrie* in Munich. August 25: Wagner marries Cosima von Bülow.
1871	First visit to Bayreuth (April). Received by Bismarck in Berlin (May 3).
1872	Leaves Triebschen and moves to Bayreuth. May 22: Wagner's 59th birthday. Foundation stone laid of Bayreuth Festival Theater.
1873	Returns to Bayreuth after concert tour.
1874	Moves into Wahnfried.
1876	August 13–17: Bayreuth Festival with first performance of the complete *Ring of the Nibelung* in the presence of Emperor Wilhelm I. October: Last meeting with Nietzsche in Sorrento.
1877	May 17: Received by Queen Victoria at Windsor.
1882	July 26: First performance of *Parsifal* at Bayreuth Festival Theater. Travels with his family to Venice.
1883	February 13: Dies at Palazzo Vendramin-Calergi, Venice. February 16: Buried in garden of Wahnfried.

BIBLIOGRAPHY

1. Letters and Other Documents

Correspondence of Wagner and Liszt. 2 vols. Edited by William Ashton Ellis. New York, revised edition, 1968.

Family Letters of Richard Wagner. London, 1911.

Letters of Richard Wagner. 2 vols. Edited by Wilhelm Altmann. New York, 1927.

Letters of Richard Wagner: The Burrell Collection. Edited by John N. Burk. New York, 1950.

My Life. 2 vols. New York, 1911.

Prose Works of Richard Wagner. 8 vols. New York, 1893–99.

Wagner on Music and Drama: A Selection from Richard Wagner's Prose Works. Arranged by Albert Goldman and Evert Spinchorn. London, 1970.

2. Biography and Criticism

BOUCHER, MAURICE. *The Political Concepts of Richard Wagner.* Translated by Marcel Honoré. New York, 1950.

ELLIS, WILLIAM ASHTON. *Life of Richard Wagner.* 6 vols. London, 1900–1908.

FINCK, HENRY T. *Wagner and His Works: The Story of His Life.* 2 vols. Westport, Conn., 1968.

FÖRSTER–NIETZSCHE, ELIZABETH. *The Nietzsche–Wagner Correspondence.* Translated by Caroline V. Kerr. New York, 1921.

GUTMAN, ROBERT W. *Richard Wagner: The Man, His Mind and His Music.* New York, 1968.

JACOBS, ROBERT L. *Wagner.* New York, 1949.

KAPP, JULIUS. *The Women in Wagner's Life.* Translated by Hannah Waller. London, 1932.

MAGEE, BRYAN. *Aspects of Wagner.* New York, 1969.

NEWMAN, ERNEST. *The Life of Richard Wagner.* 4 vols. New York, 1933–46.

————. *Wagner as Man and Artist.* New York (paper edition).

NIETZSCHE, FRIEDRICH. *The Birth of Tragedy: The Case of Wagner.* New York, 1967.

SHAW, GEORGE BERNARD. *The Perfect Wagnerite: A Commentary on the Nibelung's Ring.* New York (paper edition), 1966.

SKELTON, GEOFFREY. *Wagner at Bayreuth.* London, 1965.

STEIN, JACK M. *Richard Wagner and the Synthesis of the Arts.* Detroit, 1960.